THEMESCRIPT,
NEW PLAYS FOR NATIONAL CURR

LOYALTIES

JOHN MURRAY

ABOUT THIS BOOK

There are five playscripts in this book.

All five are about *Loyalties*.

They are about the need to stay loyal to people and ideas that you believe in.

They are about the difficult decisions you may sometimes have to make when those loyalties are threatened.

The plays have a lot of characters, so there's a good chance that everyone in the class will get to take a part.

You can read them aloud in lesson time, or rehearse them for performing to others. You'll find hints on the best ways of reading and performing in 'Using the Scripts'. If this is the first time you've used this book, we suggest that you read through the whole section.

At the end of each script, you'll also find some **Talking Points** for discussing the ideas in the play; and a list of **Investigations** with ideas for project work in English, drama, technology . . . and more.

© Series arrangement and editorial text: Alan Lambert & June Mitchell

Real Baddy © John Wood

Nora's Ark © Nona Shepphard

Jacks and Kings © Maria Oshodi

Catch-Man © Janys Chambers

Basement Bargains © Tony Coult

First published 1990
by John Murray (Publishers) Ltd
50 Albemarle St, London W1X 4BD

Cover illustration by David Anstey
Typeset by Phoenix Photosetting, Chatham, Kent
Printed and bound in Great Britain by Biddles of Guildford

British Library Cataloguing in Publication Data

Loyalties. – (Themescripts series)
   1. Drama in English, 1945 – Anthologies
   I. Series
   822. 91408

ISBN 0–7195–4804–7

CONTENTS

USING THE SCRIPTS

The playscripts have been written mainly for reading in class. Each of you can take a part or maybe share a part. They can also be learned, rehearsed and performed in front of an audience so each script has stage directions to help you present the plays.

Each play can be read straight through in about 30–40 minutes. (*Nora's Ark* is longer; it has a reading time of 50–55 minutes).

You'll find a cast list at the beginning of each script which lists the characters in the play. The characters with most to say – or those with very complicated speeches – appear first on the cast list. The cast list will also tell you whether characters are male or female. You'll find that most characters could be played by a girl or a boy without making any difference to the sense of the play.

Someone will also need to read out the stage directions (the lines in italics). These let everyone know where and when a particular scene is supposed to be taking place. They also provide a kind of linking commentary which holds the story together.

Whether you read the plays in lesson time or prepare them for performance, remember that the most important thing is to bring the script to life. It's your job to 'lift' the characters off the page and to make them talk and behave as real people.

Here are some hints that may help you in your task.

Reading Aloud

Playscripts can sometimes look very confusing. The lines are very often of different lengths and seem to be broken up more than they are in a novel or a textbook.

The characters' names are listed down the side of the page. When you're reading a character you have to read ahead a little to see when your next speech is coming up. If you don't, you'll find that there are long pauses – and maybe groans – while the rest of the class waits for you to realise that it's your turn to read. You will sometimes have time to prepare your next speech while the stage directions are being read out.

Even professional actors sometimes have difficulty in reading a script out loud when they haven't had a chance to read it first. Why should it be any easier for you? Well . . . it won't be, but there are some tricks you can use to help the reading go more smoothly, and to help the play spring into life.

4

Skip-reading

If there's time at the beginning of the lesson, start reading through the play to yourself. Even if you only manage to 'skip' through the first couple of scenes, it will give you an idea of the characters, the way they speak, the kind of language the writer is using, and the general layout of the script. You'll also begin to get some idea of the play's style. Is it funny, serious, realistic, fantastical? Is the situation one that's new to you? What are the characters like? Do you know people like them? You can discuss these points before you all get down to reading the play together. Ten minutes' skip-reading will lead to a more lively and enjoyable session.

You can skip-read with a partner, each of you taking alternate lines. If there was time you could probably work your way through the entire play like this.

Searching out the tricky bits

You'll need preparation time for this too. Instead of skip-reading the opening scenes, flick through the entire play. Watch out for any difficult or unfamiliar words. If you've already been given a character to read, just go through your own lines. Otherwise, help out with a general search and don't forget to watch out for tricky stage directions.

Occasionally the play will ask your character to sing a song. Sing it if you know the tune, but otherwise read it out as if it were a poem.

Quick character sketches

If you've never seen these plays before, how can you find out about the character you've been asked to read? You'll find some help in the cast list at the start of each script. As you read you'll obviously get to know more about him or her; the speeches will give you clues as to what the character is like. You can also get help from your teacher. The chances are that they will know the script well and may have used it with other groups before.

Ask about your character. Maybe even ask for a demonstration of how your teacher sees the character. How would they begin to play it?

Reading ahead

Learn the trick of reading ahead . . . of letting your eyes move on a couple of lines when another character is speaking, so that you're ready with your speech when your turn comes.

This is not always easy because you've still got to concentrate on what other people are saying. If you don't, you're likely to lose your place completely. With practice, though, you may find yourself becoming a very smooth play reader.

You'll also need to use the same kind of skill when you're reading a speech that carries over from one line to the next. Don't pause at the end of the line *unless* it is also the end of a sentence, otherwise it will make for a real stop–start performance.

Watching for signals

As you read ahead you'll also need to watch for the signals the writer gives you on how to read your lines.

So when you see commas and full stops don't be afraid to pause. Dashes '–' or a series of dots '. . .' also mean you should pause. Don't be shy about giving real feeling to a sentence that ends with an exclamation mark! Where a writer tells you that a character whispers . . . whisper. Where you read that a character shouts . . . SHOUT!

In *Catch-Man* you will also need to notice question marks as well, because the way the characters speak in that play means it isn't always obvious what is a question and what is a statement.

Enjoy making your speeches lively or dramatic or funny or frightened . . . or whatever it is they're supposed to be. Put as much expression as you can into the reading, because if *you* do, the chances are that you'll encourge your classmates to do the same. Plays are meant for sharing.

Looking forwards and backwards

It can be very useful to stop the reading for a few seconds at a suitable moment and discuss together as a class what you think is going to happen next. For example, in *Nora's Ark* on page 65 you could discuss whether you think the young people will decide to go with Nora or not. In the same way, after some complicated action you can pause to discuss what has happened so far.

Second readings

Once you're through the first reading, and if you've enjoyed what the play is saying – or even if there are ideas there that you don't yet understand – there's the possibility of a second reading.

You may not want to go through the whole play but perhaps there are one or two sections that you'd like to read again or deal with in greater detail. A second reading also gives you the chance to swap the parts around.

Performing the Plays

Some people enjoy performing a play to an audience; on the other hand, some people hate the idea!

If you've only got a limited amount of time to get a performance ready, it will be better to choose just one or two scenes and really concentrate on doing these well.

For some performances you'll need to write to the publishers for permission. Details are at the beginning of this book.

If you decide to prepare one of these scripts for performance, then you'll need to give some thought to the kind of performance it's going to be.

Here are some of your choices.

Performing 'live': making a piece of theatre

If you're going to make a 'live' performance where are you going to present it? On a stage? In the round – with the audience sitting on all sides of the acting area? In a corner of a classroom?

Are you going to have elaborate settings and costumes, or will you keep the whole event very simple? Most of the plays in this book allow for very simple staging.

Are you going to have stage lighting? If so, would this be the most effective way of changing scenes?

You could do a rehearsed reading. You don't need to learn the lines and work out moves for this because you sit and read the play to your audience. But go through the play several times together first, so that you can give the reading real expression!

Making a video play

If you have the use of a video camera, can you adapt the script for showing as a television play? If so, will you simply point the camera at the scene, or will you want to experiment with close-ups and long shots and camera angles? Will you need to rewrite the script as a 'shooting script'?

As with a live performance, you'll have to think about the kind of settings and costumes you're going to use. Will you need to film 'on location' to give your presentation the kind of realistic feel that looks good on television? Some of the plays in this collection lend themselves well to location work; there are scenes set in classrooms, playgrounds, houses and streets. You may find it more difficult, though, to track down an appropriate location for *Catch-Man* or even *Basement Bargains*; but if you feel like taking up the challenge, why not try?

Making a radio play

Recording a play on tape looks the simplest choice of all. Certainly you won't have to worry about costumes, settings, lighting or complicated moves. But there are some details that you ought to bear in mind as you prepare for this type of presentation.

How many microphones are you going to use? Where are you going to position them to get the best effect? Remember that your actors need to be able to get to a microphone easily when it's their turn to speak.

Have you got a recording room where you can keep out unwanted sounds? Will you want to record 'on location'? Some of the plays would make for very realistic-sounding radio productions if you were able to record them in and around your school and neighbourhood.

Do any of your actors' voices sound the same? If so you may be heading for trouble because your listeners won't be able to tell which character is speaking. Choose a range of voices to make for variety and to avoid confusion.

So . . . what kind of presentation will you choose to make? One advantage of the video and radio versions is that they can often be less nerve-racking for those people who don't like getting up and performing in front of an audience. And for those people who can't even stand the sight of themselves on video, the radio play has got to be the best choice of all!

Whichever you choose, the actor's job is to make the piece come to life. The words on the paper need to be given flesh and blood – *yours!* In the time that you've got available, do as much work as you can on your character. How do they look and sound? What's their history? What kind of place do they live in? Do you know anyone who looks or acts like them?

If you don't want to act, you could be a director, stage manager, camera operator, musician, sound recordist, costume maker, designer, lighting operator, publicity manager . . . These jobs are just as important as the actors in bringing the play to life, and making a success of the final product.

There's a lot of effort involved in getting a play ready for performance. It requires a great deal of co-operation from everyone. But at the end of it all, you may find that there's a real BUZZ in it – for both you and your audience.

REAL BADDY

John Wood

THE CHARACTERS

Michael Crockton, known to his mates as Crocky
Janet, a friend
Patch Eye Cook, the local tramp (male)
Mr Briggs, headmaster
Mr Crockton, Michael's father
PC Bell, sometimes known as 'Ding Dong' Bell

Crocky's classmates:

Susan
Bev
Mandy
Tommy
Tubby (male)
Billy

Janet's mother
Janet's father
Frankie, Janet's younger brother

About this play

Real Baddy is based on a true story. It's the 1950s, in a small town in the north of England. It's the kind of town where everyone knows everyone else, and if you've got a reputation, you're stuck with it for life. Like Crocky! He's got a reputation as a 'real baddy': people say he's always in trouble. So, when a shovel gets stolen from the local mill, Crocky gets the blame. This time, though, he decides that he's not going to stick around and get punished for something he hasn't done. With the help of his friend Janet, he goes into hiding.

SCENE 1

*(The living room of a council house. In the corner of the room there is a
large television set, which shows that this family is not short of money.
Mr Crockton stands in the centre of the room. His son, **Michael**, has
just arrived home – late. He is pale and near to tears . . .)*

Mr Crockton   Where have you been? It's dark outside.

*(**Crocky** is silent . . . but he looks as if he's going to cry.)*

Mr Crockton   I asked you where you've been. And don't start
crying.

Crocky   I'm not.

Mr Crockton   So where have you been? Don't lie. Your mother's
been going frantic.

Crocky   It's only eight o'clock.

Mr Crockton   That's not the point is it? It's dark! Well . . . I'm
waiting?

Crocky   I ran all the way. I'm sorry.

Mr Crockton   Sorry! How many times have we heard that? Sorry
for pinching out of your mum's purse; sorry for bullying at
school; sorry for stealing from shops; sorry for being on
probation. We're fed up with your 'sorries'. What have you
been up to this time?

Crocky   I haven't been up to anything.

Mr Crockton   Makes a change doesn't it? Where have you been?
What have you been doing?

Crocky   Just messing about. I haven't been doing anything.

*(**Crocky** fights back his tears.)*

Mr Crockton   Don't start blubbing. It's always the same isn't it;
give Michael Crockton an inch and he takes you for a ride. *I* was
supposed to be down at the club half an hour ago.

Crocky   You won't let me have the watch Gran gave me.

Mr Crockton   That's a punishment. When you start considering other people you get it back.

Crocky   But without my watch I never know what time it is.

Mr Crockton   You know when it's getting dark.

Crocky   I ran all the way.

Mr Crockton   You were late. Go and apologise to your mother, she's lying down upstairs. And bring down the slipper.

Crocky   I won't be late again. I promise. Dad, I'm sorry.

Mr Crockton   You should have thought of that before. You've upset your mother and you've made me miss my darts match.

Crocky   I promise. I promise.

Mr Crockton   Get that slipper or I'll use the stick!

Crocky   I haven't been bad. I haven't. Gran knows.

Mr Crockton   So, that's where you've been!

Crocky   She met me from school.

Mr Crockton   You were told not to see her the whole of this week.

Crocky   She met me.

Mr Crockton   A punishment is a punishment. You agreed not to see her and to be home on time. You failed on both.

Crocky   Gran said –

Mr Crockton   I don't care what she said. You're my son and you'll do as I say. She's not bringing you up. I am. So you'll do as you're told, understand? Get upstairs and fetch that slipper.

Crocky   Please, please, I haven't been bad.

(**Mr Crockton** *picks up the nearest ornament and smashes it on the floor.* **Crocky** *has seen this behaviour before and knows that it will end with his father using the slipper.*)

Mr Crockton   Stop crying. No son of mine cries. You never learn, do you? Get that slipper.

(*Shaking,* **Crocky** *goes upstairs.*)

SCENE 2

(The next day: at the school railings. **Crocky** *and* **Tommy Hayes** *are standing in the playground, looking out on to the main road where a bearded, scruffy man with a patch over one eye is unsuccessfully trying to direct the traffic.)*

Tommy   Look at Patch Eye Cook. Thinks he's directing traffic. Idiot! Shall we brick him?

Crocky   Naah, he'll get run over in a minute. Squashed Patch Eye Cook pancakes *(He shouts.)* Squash me and fry one!

*(***Tommy*** *joins in the taunting.)*

Tommy   Got your eye in, Patch Eye?

Crocky   Look both ways at once! Yeh!

*(***Patch Eye*** *shouts back.)*

Patch Eye   I know you. I get you.

Both   Yaaah.

Crocky   See his head go.

*(***Crocky*** *mimics the way* ***Patch Eye*** *moves his head from side to side to see the traffic with his one eye.)*

Tommy   Like a chicken isn't he?

*(***Mr Briggs,*** *the headmaster, appears behind them.)*

Mr Briggs   Didn't you two hear the bell?

Tommy   Sorry sir.

Mr Briggs   On your way, Hayes.

*(***Tommy*** *goes.)*

Mr Briggs   Crockton, I want a word with you. Were you in the old mill yesterday? Don't bother lying. You were seen. A shovel's been stolen. Tell your father to come up to the school tomorrow. I'm fed up with your petty pilfering.

Crocky   I haven't nicked no shovel.

Mr Briggs   Wherever you are, things go missing. Mostly valuable things.

Crocky   It wasn't me.

Mr Briggs   Nothing's ever you. Were you there yesterday?

Crocky   I didn't nick anything.

Mr Briggs   The mill is private property. You've no right to go over there. Tell your father nine o'clock, and you can tell him that if I have my way this is the end of your career in this school. Get along to your class.

(Crocky moves off towards Tommy. Mr Briggs turns his attention to Patch Eye Cook.)

Mr Briggs *(shouting)*   You, get off that road; you'll get yourself killed.

Patch Eye   I'm not one of yer kids, yer red-haired git.

Tommy   Briggs is going to murder Patch Eye. Look at him. Stupid old dosser.

(They walk up towards the classrooms. Crocky is obviously worried.)

Tommy   Why did you nick a shovel?

(Crocky hits him.)

Tommy   Ow. What's that for?

Crocky   Get lost, Hayes.

(Tommy Hayes goes into the classroom. Crocky looks back to where Patch Eye and Briggs are having an argument in the middle of the road.)

Crocky *(shouting)*   You tell him, Patch Eye!

SCENE 3

(The same day; a classroom in the second break. Crocky's encounter with Briggs has gone round the school {courtesy of Tommy} with everyone adding their own bit to the story.

Susan is sitting on a desk eating a bag of crisps. Her best mate, Bev, is drilling a hole in the desk with a penknife. Janet comes in, moves over to the window and opens it.)

Janet   Smells in here.

Susan (*talking loudly to* **Bev** *who just smiles in reply*)   Have you heard what Michael Crockton's been up to? He nicked a dumper full of tools from over the Old Mill. Briggs is getting the police in. Fingerprints and everything. Didn't you know?

Janet   Didn't you know your tongue's hanging out? It must be loose.

Susan   Funny ha ha.

Janet   It will be if you don't keep out of other people's business.

Susan   He's going to get done. About time too. He's a real baddy if you ask me.

Janet   No one is asking you. So shut it, Hickmott.

Susan   Don't know why you're so bothered. He don't fancy you from what I've heard.

Janet   He doesn't fancy you, gobby.

Susan   Sticks and stones. Stuck-up cow.

Janet   Give it a rest. Leave him alone for once, hey?

Susan (*chanting the words of a popular song*)   On and on it will always be, true love, true love.

   (*She and* **Bev** *dissolve into laughter.*)

Janet   I hope someone hurts *you* one day.

   (*The bell sounds, covering* **Susan's** *reply.*)

SCENE 4

   (*After school.* **Crocky** *and* **Janet** *are sitting on their bikes on the iron bridge. It's a 'no cycling area'. Beneath them a fast-flowing stream ripples over pebbles. They are both gazing down.*)

Crocky   What would I want a shovel for? I get blamed for everything.

Janet   You could write to the paper.

Crocky It's not fair. Just 'cos they saw me. Could have been anyone. My old man's going to go wild.

Janet We could go and nick one from somewhere else.

Crocky An get done for nicking *two* shovels? Thanks!

Janet I'll nick one and say I found it.

Crocky I'll bet they'll believe that. Briggs said next time I got in trouble it'd be the last. It's not fair. What makes him think he's always right?

Janet He's a teacher.

Crocky My old man's going to kill me if I go home.

Janet Don't go then. Hide.

Crocky Then he'll kill me for not going home. Great!

Janet No, I mean hide out until they realise you're innocent. There's the empty house behind the Co-op. You can stay there and I'll find out who took that shovel. Someone will know.

Crocky He'll kill me if I don't go home.

Janet At least you'd be in trouble for something you've done, instead of for something you didn't do!

Crocky Yeh!

Janet There's a little room in the attic, no one would ever find you up there.

Crocky I'd need a candle, matches, blanket , , ,

Janet Tin opener . . .

Crocky . . . Food. You're right. I'm not getting done for this; not when I didn't do it. They aren't getting me. Don't tell anyone. Promise?

Janet Promise.

Crocky You get that stuff. See you there later. When you get to the top of the stairs whistle three times, then I'll know it's you.

Janet OK. Look out. Get off your bike. It's Dinger Bell.

(A policeman pushes his bike over the bridge as it is a no cycling area.)

Bell   Not about to ride that bike were you, Crockton? Know better than that, even you. I'm popping in to see your father later about a certain matter. Never learn, do you? Have you thought how you're going to get a job with a reputation like yours? No. You'll end up like all the other lads in this town who haven't listened – you'll end up in a remand home and they'll sort you out. Tell your father to expect me. Now, on your way – walking.

Crocky   See you Jan.

Janet   See you.

*(**Crocky** moves off whistling defiantly. **Bell** shakes his head and turns to **Janet**.)*

Bell   Do your mother and father know you're hanging about with him?

Janet   I just met him. We go to the same school you know.

Bell   He's always in trouble. A bad lot. There's plenty of nice lads about. Don't be a fool to yourself. I won't say anything to your father this time.

Janet *(sarcastically)*   Thanks.

Bell   You were brought up to be more polite than that.

Janet   Thank you.

Bell   Where's the top off your bell?

Janet   They nick them at school.

Bell   Get one by Saturday. Push your bike home, it's too dark to ride now with no lights.

Janet   They nick *them* too if you take them to school.

Bell   Have you ever thought who might be nicking them?

*(He indicates the direction **Crocky** went in.)*

Janet   No.

Bell   Walk on the pavement, we don't want you getting run over.

(He walks off.)

Janet *(as loud as she dare)*   Ding Dong Bell
   Pussy's in the well
   Who'll get it out
   Dinger if you shout
   Ding Dong Bell
   Ding Dong Bell
   Ding Dong Bell!

SCENE 5

*(An hour later, in the empty house. It is dark. **Crocky** is waiting for **Janet** on the top floor. He hears a noise in the darkness and the sound of footsteps coming up the stairs. They stop outside the room where he is hiding and then they enter.)*

Crocky   Jan. You're supposed to whistle. Jan? *(No reply.)* I've got a knife. Who's there? I'm not scared of you.

Patch Eye   I seen knives. I seen some long knives.

Crocky   Patch Eye Cook, you old dosser. You're mad.

Patch Eye   What's madder than an adder? An adder what can't add.

Crocky   Push off. This is my place. Find your own.

Patch Eye   Who you hiding from?

Crocky   No one.

Patch Eye   What you afraid of?

Crocky   Nothing.

Patch Eye   Is that so? Is that so?

Crocky   Yeh. Sling yer hook.

*(**Patch Eye** lights a match. **Crocky** is outlined on the floor under the trapdoor leading to the attic room.)*

Patch Eye   Let's see your face.

Crocky   You tell anyone you seen me and you're dead. Got it? Dead.

Patch Eye   Give us a shilling.

Crocky   No.

(**Patch Eye** *blows out the match and starts reciting a poem.*)

Patch Eye   'I see your lights he cried, but ours had long since died.' War! You never get what they promise you. Remember that boy.

Crocky   I told you, I got a knife.

Patch Eye   You stay here. You don't have to go to war. That's how it should be when you're young. They should leave you alone.

(*He leaves. His shuffling footsteps are very distinct on the stair until at last he has gone and the house again becomes silent.*)

Crocky   Silly old sod.

(*He closes the trapdoor.*)

SCENE 6

(**Janet's** *house: nine o'clock that evening. Her* **mother** *is washing up the supper things and has already broken a plate. The* **father** *comes in late wanting to know why* **Janet** *has been allowed out at this time of night . . .*)

Father   Why's she had to go out? Where's she gone?

Frankie   Where's my pyjamas?

Mother   She's taken some book round to Carol's.

Frankie   Mum, where's my pyjamas?

Father   I don't like her gallivanting about at this time of night.

Frankie   I can't find them Mum.

Mother   Then get home early enough so you can tell her.

Father   Why don't *you* tell her?

Mother   I'm too busy looking after the other children. She's old enough to look after herself.

Father   No daughter of mine –

Mother Listen to you!

Frankie Found them!!

Mother If you want to bring the children up you have to be here, not there!

Father Where?

Mother Wherever it is you've been.

Father I had to go out – business.

Mother So did she – her business.

Father Why'd you let her go?

Mother Because I can't do everything! You expect too much. I can't do it all. I can't. I can't.

Father All right. All right.

Frankie The cat's done poo poos.

Father Where? (*Frankie points.*) Oh God. We'll clear it up in a minute. (*To Janet's **Mother**.*) Where do you think she's gone?

(*Janet's **Mother** shakes her head.*)

SCENE 7

(*The house behind the Co-op. **Janet** makes her way up the stairs. She shines a bicycle lamp on the trapdoor to the attic and gives three low whistles. The trapdoor opens and **Crocky's** head appears.*)

Crocky You took your time!

Janet I had to help Mum.

(***Crocky** jumps down from the trapdoor.*)

Janet There's tinned rice, a tin opener, and a spoon. I pinched the blanket off the dog.

Crocky Thanks.

Janet It's not easy, you know. I've gotta get back.

Crocky Leave the lamp.

Janet OK. But I'll have to scoot most of the way, Dinger already warned me about no lights. You all right?

Crocky Yeh.

Janet You don't sound it.

Crocky Well I am.

Janet Spooky isn't it?

Crocky I want something to drink. There's no water in here.

Janet I'll bring a bottle of milk in the morning. Got to go. My mum was dead suspicious. See ya.

Crocky See ya.

(*He shines the lamp down the stairs lighting the way out. She turns at the door and waves. He is left alone. He shines the lamp around the bare walls and down on to the little pile of things* **Janet** *has brought.*)

Crocky Pigging shovel!

SCENE 8

(**Janet** *reaches home, puts her bike around the back and enters by the kitchen door. Her* **Father** *and* **Mother** *are waiting.*)

Father Where have you been?

Janet Round Carol's.

Mother You said you wouldn't be long.

Janet I've only been half an hour. She wanted help with her German. Where do you think I've been?

Father We don't know.

Janet Well, I've been round Carol's.

Father Will you swear to that?

Mother I think she's telling the truth, Geoff.

Father Will you?

Janet Yes.

Father   On the Bible.

Mother   Geoff!

Father   Will you swear on the Holy Book that you've been out to
Carol's tonight?

Janet (*a pause*)   Yes.

Mother   You're a good girl, Janet.

Janet   I'm going to bed or do you want me to swear that's where
I'm going as well?

(*She turns and swanks up the stairs, but in reality her legs are shaking
and she is hoping that crossing both fingers will have saved her from
eternal damnation.*)

SCENE 9

(*Next morning, in assembly. The hymn 'O God our help in ages past' is
just finishing.* **Susan, Janet, Bev** and **Mandy** stand in a line,
whispering to each other.)

Susan   Where's Crocky today then? Lovesick?

Janet   Shut up Susan.

Mr Briggs (*calls out from the stage*)   The Lord's prayer!

Susan   Or is he too scared to come to school?

Janet   Our Father which art in Heaven.

Susan   Coward be thy name.

Janet   Leave it out.

(*She nudges* **Mandy** *who stumbles against* **Bev.**)

Mandy   Don't push me!

Bev   Who's pushing?

Susan   It's her.

Bev   Do you want trouble?

Janet   Don't interfere Bev. It's none of your business.

Bev   It is if I'm getting pushed.

Mandy   You tell her Bev.

Janet   Shut up you little squirt.

Mandy   She can't talk to me like that, can she Bev?

Susan   There's no boy to hide behind now.

(*Janet* pushes **Susan** *violently.* **Mandy** *falls onto* **Bev**.)

Mandy   Give her one, Bev.

Mr Briggs   What is going on over there? Watkins, Mawdsley, Hickmott and the other girl. If you have no respect for God, you'll not be surprised to learn that I shall have little respect for you. Outside my office NOW!

SCENE 10

(*Later, in the corridor outside the head's office. The girls wait for* **Mr Briggs** *to arrive.*)

Mandy   Stupid!

Bev   Shut up Mandy.

Susan   I'm not taking the blame. It was you lot started shoving.

Mandy   No it wasn't.

Bev   Tell them it was your high heels.

Janet   Why don't you three club together and buy yourselves a cage – bird brains.

(*Three boys come down the corridor:* **Tubby, Tommy** *and* **Billy**.)

Tubby   You tell them scarecrow.

Bev   Where's Crocky then?

Susan   'Please, sir, it wasn't me sir.'

Billy   Put your face in a comic Hickmott.

Susan   Where'd you get yours?

Bev   Off the back of a bus.

Mandy Where is he then?

Tommy Wouldn't you like to know?

Susan Where is he?

Tommy We don't split on a mate.

Bev He daren't come to school.

Billy That's where you're wrong, Bev. He doesn't want to come in.

Tubby Better things to do.

Susan Such as?

Janet Wouldn't you like to know?

Bev Yeh.

(*Mr Briggs comes down the corridor.*)

Mr Briggs Mickulick, Turner, Hayes, in my office now!

Tubby Sir, we haven't done nothing.

Mr Briggs I want to see you three now.

Tubby What about them?

Mr Briggs They can wait, Mickulick. It's you three I want to see, now. Inside.

(*He opens the door and sweeps in. The three boys reluctantly follow.*)

Mandy You're for it.

Tommy Shut up ugly.

(*The door shuts.*)

SCENE 11

(*In **Mr Briggs's** office. He faces the boys.*)

Mr Briggs You're all friends of Crockton's. His little gang. Don't lie. Where is he?

Tubby Don't know sir.

Mr Briggs You're not in Maths now, Mickulick. Where is he?

Tubby   I haven't seen him sir. Don't know where he is.

Mr Briggs   Would you like to tell his father that? Well?

Tubby   I don't know, sir.

Mr Briggs   His father wants to know where he is. He hasn't seen him since yesterday. He's not been home. Who's hiding him? Turner?

Billy   No sir.

Mr Briggs   Hayes?

Tommy   No sir.

Mr Briggs   What about you, Mickulick? – 'Don't know, sir?'

Tubby   No, sir.

Mr Briggs   Look, this isn't a lark, it's serious. If you know where he is I want to know. *(He waits.)* All right, have it your own way. But if I find out you've been lying, and I *will* find out, God help you all. Out. Send the other lot in here.

SCENE 12

*(In the corridor, the boys troop out of **Mr Briggs's** office. The girls have been listening at the door.)*

Tubby   He wants you in there.

Susan   So Crocky *has* run away.

Mandy   Cowardy! I said he had.

Janet   You don't know anything about anything.

Mr Briggs *(coming out of his office)*   No talking. Off to your classes, boys. Now young ladies, come in here and explain why the Word of God is less important than the babblings of Form Two girls. Enter.

(The girls go in. The door shuts behind them. The boys are left trying to work out whether their hero is a coward or not.)

Billy   He's done it this time.

Tommy   Done what?

Billy   Not come to school.

Tubby   He's run away.

Tommy   He hasn't run away, Crocky wouldn't run away, not without telling us.

Tubby   Where is he then?

Tommy *(in an American accent)*   He's waiting for the heat to cool.

Tubby   Do you have to talk American?

Billy   He didn't go home, we know that.

Tommy   We know nothing. That's what he wants us to know. Nothing. So that's what we know. OK?

Billy   This isn't a stupid film. It's serious. Nobody knows where he is, not even his parents. He could be dead you know.

(With that sobering thought they wander off to Maths.)

SCENE 13

(The same day, on the top floor of the empty house.
Time is beginning to pass slowly for **Crocky** *and he's still cold from the previous night. He starts to lean out from the top windows and watch delivery lorries moving to and fro in the Co-op yard. Then he sees* **Patch Eye Cook** *coming towards the house.* **Crocky** *moves to the top of the stairs, and sits there, whistling.*
Patch Eye *comes in eating a bag of chips.)*

Crocky   What are you doing back here?

Patch Eye   Chips. You hungry? You have some.

Crocky   Not if you've had your dirty mits round them.

Patch Eye   Four penn'orth – in paper.

Crocky   Why are you giving them me? You put something on them?

Patch Eye   Salt and vinegar.

Crocky   You're daft as a brush, you. Where did you sleep last night?

Patch Eye   On the common. Air raid shelter.

Crocky   Bit breezy weren't it? I thought the roof was blowing off here. Good at night on your own ain't it? You ever get scared?

*(**Patch Eye** just smiles. **Crocky** stuffs a handful of chips into his mouth and begins to realise how hungry he was.)*

Crocky   Always on about the war aren't you? You ever kill anyone?

Patch Eye   What I do in the war, I told to do. I told to shoot. To kill.

Crocky   Great!

Patch Eye   I told to shoot prisoners.

Crocky   Why'd they have to be shot? Why'd you shoot them?

Patch Eye   They don't tell us their secrets. My army, they say 'shoot prisoners who don't talk'. But if I prisoner and I talk, my army would say 'traitor'. How can I shoot soldiers who won't tell secrets? But if I don't obey my orders my army shoot me. So I shoot prisoners.

Crocky   That's bad.

Patch Eye   That is war. I tell *you* secret . . . Never give yourself up, nobody don't respect you if you give up, call you coward, treat you bad, hit you, shoot you maybe. Never give up. Damn fool thing to do. Keep fighting. You understand?

*(**Crocky** nods and he eats the rest of the chips in silence.)*

Crocky   Thanks for the chips.

Patch Eye   Fourpence you owe me.

Crocky   Not all daft are you? What you got in there? Ciggies?

Patch Eye   Cards. You play game?

Crocky   What game?

Patch Eye   I show you. Seven cards. We play all the time in war.

*(**Patch Eye** starts to deal the cards.)*

SCENE 14

*(A school classroom. **Mr Briggs, PC Bell** and **Mr Crockton** are talking to Crocky's classmates.)*

Mr Briggs You've all heard by now that Michael Crockton is missing. It seems reasonable to assume that his disappearance is in some way connected with events already being investigated by myself and PC Bell.

Tommy *(very quietly)* Ding Dong.

Mr Briggs Events that some of you may have a more intimate knowledge of than others. However, as you can see, Michael's father has come along to say a few words to you as a class. After he's spoken, myself and PC Bell −

Tommy Ding Dong.

Mr Briggs − will see each of you separately. We will want to know three things, Hayes.

Tommy Yes sir.

Mr Briggs The last time you saw Michael; what you spoke about; and what you can tell us that might give us a clue as to where he is. Mr Crockton.

Bev I wouldn't let my dad come in to school.

Mr Crockton Mick's got into some bad company, I know that.

Bev Yeh.

Mr Crockton He's not a bad lad. He helps his Gran a lot.

*(**Bev** holds back laughter.)*

Tommy Shut up Bev.

Mr Briggs What's the matter with you, Beverly?

Bev I was trying not to sneeze sir. Sorry, Mr Crockton.

Mr Crockton His mum's worried sick. She's had to have the doctor. Whatever's happened in the past, whether you're a friend of his or not, try and help. If he's given you a pasting, don't let it stop you telling. What you know might help. A few hits ain't nothing now he's gone missing. Thanks.

Tommy   See.

Bev   All right.

Mr Briggs   I hope you take that to heart. Think about his mother. Alphabetical order outside my office. Boothroyd, Mandy.

*(The adults start to leave the room. **Mandy** gets up to follow.)*

Mandy   What do I tell them Bev?

Billy   Your bra size, brainless.

Mandy   Something *you'll* never know, maggot.

(She goes.)

Tommy   I've been thinking. You know where he was when I saw him last? We were shouting at Patch Eye Cook, and Patch Eye threatened to get us.

Tubby   You better tell Ding Dong.

Billy   No. Let's go and find Patch Eye first.

Tommy   Yeh. We'll make him talk.

SCENE 15

*(Inside the house. **Crocky** and **Patch Eye** are still playing cards. **Patch Eye** has heard **Crocky's** story and knows what it is like to be picked on unfairly. He understands that even if **Crocky** has done a few bad things that doesn't make him altogether 'a bad person'. He looks for the nice bits, and consequently **Crocky** and he are getting on well together.)*

Crocky   Spades again.

(There's a noise outside.)

Patch Eye   Ssh. Listen. Outside. Get up there.

*(He points to the attic trapdoor. **Crocky** climbs on a chair and pulls himself up, into the attic.)*

Crocky   Whistle three times for all clear.

Patch Eye   No teeth. I call you. What's your name?

Crocky   Crocky. No splitting, heh?

Patch Eye   I no tell. We soldiers. Mates? Yeh?

Crocky   Yeh.

(**Crocky** *climbs up through the trapdoor and closes it.* **Patch Eye** *goes downstairs.*)

SCENE 16

(*Outside the empty house.* **Patch Eye** *comes through the doorway and walks across the wasteground. From behind a wall* **Billy**, **Tommy** *and* **Tubby** *step out armed with sticks.*)

Tommy   Gotcha. Where's Crocky?

Billy   Our mate.

Tubby   Dinger Bell knows you threatened him.

Billy   You stink.

Patch Eye   You his friends?

Billy   Yeah.

Patch Eye   Then you should know where he is.

Tommy   I told you. Don't move.

Tubby   You're going to see Ding Dong. He wants to talk to you.

Billy   You dirty old dosser.

Tommy   Get going. If you don't talk you get one of these.

(**Tommy** *hits him with a stick.*)

Tommy   Talk!

Billy   Or else.

Tubby   We'll kill you.

Patch Eye   Prisoner of war. No talk.

Billy   Don't be stupid. (*He hits him.*) Where's Crocky?

Tubby (*hits him*)   Where is he?

Tommy Talk.

Patch Eye No.

Billy We'll kill you.

Tommy Get going you old stinkbag.

(*They push him along with their sticks.*)

SCENE 17

(*In the classroom.* **Mr Briggs, Mr Crockton** *and* **PC Bell** *are standing around* **Janet** *who is sitting on a chair.*)

Bell You've not been entirely honest with us have you Janet?

Janet Yes.

Bell You're the last person to have talked to him. I know, I saw you. You also said you 'just happened to meet him'.

Janet So?

Mr Briggs It's not true is it? Other people say you left school together.

Bell You're his friend.

Janet Not a crime is it?

Mr Crockton Where is he?

Janet What do you want to know for? So you can give him another good hiding?

Bell So you do know where he is.

Janet If I did I wouldn't tell you.

Mr Briggs Janet, you're not in any trouble yet . . . Where did you say he was going?

Janet I don't know.

Mr Briggs Your classmates say that you do a lot together.

Janet Do they?

Bell And your parents don't know, do they?

Janet   Know what?

Mr Crockton   That you're hiding my son.

Mr Briggs   They wouldn't approve of him, would they?

Janet   There's nothing wrong with him.

Mr Crockton   Apart from his reputation. Where is he?

Mr Briggs   Everyone knows that you know where he is.

Bell   What will your parents say?

Mr Crockton   I know what I'd do with her if she were my girl.

Janet   Give me a good belting. That's all you know, isn't it? Why d'you think he wouldn't go home? 'Cos of you. You're all the same. Always on his back, whether he's done anything or not. He didn't nick that shovel.

Mr Briggs   We know. (*He looks at* **PC Bell**.) It's been found. (*Then to* **Janet**.) It was all a bit of a mistake.

Bell   Yes. Someone jumped to a hasty conclusion, I'm afraid. He's not going to get into trouble for that, is he Mr Crockton? Or anything else.

Mr Crockton   No. (*Pause.*) All we want is to see him home, his mother and me. He's had enough punishment.

Mr Briggs   It would be a relief for him to hear that, wouldn't it Janet? Where is he?

(**Janet** *shakes her head.*)

Mr Crockton   I know I've been a bit hard on him, but I'm not asking this for myself. I'm asking you, begging you, for his mum's sake – she cried her eyes out last night.

Mr Briggs   If Michael knew that, don't you think he'd want to go home?

Bell   Will you go and tell him, Janet? Tell him it's all been a mistake. Will you do that? Your parents needn't know you've been mixed up with him. Isn't that right, sir?

Mr Briggs   No need to know at all.

Mr Crockton   Nobody's going to hurt him. Take us to him. I want to say 'sorry'.

Bell   We've all been a bit hasty in judging him.

Mr Briggs   But it's all over now.

Mr Crockton   Please Janet; will you take us to him, for his mother's sake?

(*Janet nods.*)

Bell   You're a good girl.

Mr Briggs   Where is he?

Janet   In the empty house behind the Co-op.

Bell   I've checked that.

Janet   He's in the attic. I have to whistle three times.

Mr Briggs   I'll get my car.

(*There are shouts from the playground.* **Mr Briggs** *goes to the window and looks down.*)

Mr Briggs   It's that damned tramp. (*He shouts down.*) Leave him alone. Clear off! Tell him to go.

(**Tommy** *calls from outside.*)

Tommy   Sir! He knows where Crocky is, sir.

Patch Eye   I never tell, you red-haired git. We soldiers. We don't tell. Never.

Mr Briggs   Get rid of him.

Tommy   But he knows, sir.

Mr Briggs   So do I. We're going to get him!

(*On hearing this* **Patch Eye** *leaps on* **PC Bell's** *bike and cycles off, chased by the three boys.*)

Mr Briggs   He's taken your bike, PC Bell.

Bell   I'll have his guts for garters!

Mr Briggs   He causes more trouble round here than − than anyone else. Let's go shall we? We'll use my car.

Bell You're a good girl, Janet. You've done the right thing.

SCENE 18

*(On the wasteground, outside the empty house. **Mr Briggs, Mr Crockton** and **PC Bell** have arrived by car with **Janet**. They stand, looking up at the house.)*

Bell You go first, Janet, and call him down from the attic. We'll be waiting outside the room.

Mr Briggs *(whispers to **Bell**)* What if he tries to run for it?

Bell *(looks up at the house)* He'll be on the second floor. We'll have the doors covered. He'd have to grow wings. Come on, Janet. Quietly does it.

(They go into the house.)

SCENE 19

*(On the top floor. **Janet** quietly comes up the staircase and moves to a spot underneath the trapdoor leading to the attic. The adults are ready to block the doors when **Crocky** comes down and so trap him in the room . . . **Janet** whistles three times, then whispers . . .)*

Janet Crocky. Crocky.

*(**Crocky** opens the trapdoor and jumps down.)*

Crocky What are you doing here? Why aren't you at school? Have you seen Patch Eye? What's wrong?

*(The adults appear in the doorway. **Crocky** looks at **Janet**, his face twisting with contempt.)*

Crocky You . . .

Mr Crockton It's all right, Michael. We're going home.

*(**Crocky** puts his head down and runs at what everyone, including him, believes to be a solid brick wall. Just like in a comic he bursts through it — it was made of plasterboard.*

*Before the adults have recovered from their surprise he has jumped out of a window in the next room and landed heavily on the porch roof above the front door. The adults and **Janet** run to watch from the window. They are joined by **Patch Eye**, who has just arrived – breathless.)*

Mr Briggs   He's jumped on the roof of the porch.

Mr Crockton   Michael. Stay where you are.

Patch Eye   Jump!

*(**Tubby**, **Billy** and **Tommy** arrive to see **Crocky** leap from the roof. They cheer.)*

Mr Crockton   He has! The idiot.

Mr Briggs   Stop that boy!

*(**Mr Briggs**, **Mr Crockton** and **PC Bell** turn and race down the stairs.*
   Patch Eye shouts from the window.)

Patch Eye   Run! Run! They never catch you.

Tubby   Take Ding Dong's bike.

Billy   Over there! By the wall!

*(**Crocky** pedals off as the others continue to watch from the window and shout encouragements.)*

Tubby   He's pinched it!

Billy . Look at him go. Go, Crocky, go!!

Tubby   Yeh.

Janet   They'll never catch him now.

Patch Eye   No. Never.

Tommy   Mind you, I'd hate to be him when they do.

*(**Bell** runs back up the stairs and confronts them.)*

Bell   We missed him. Which way did he go?

*(**Patch Eye** looks at **Janet** and the boys. There is a silent agreement that they are going to lie. **Patch Eye** points in the wrong direction.)*

(This story is based on fact. In real life the boy jumped out of the window and broke his leg but kept running for a mile until finally he was caught.)

Talking Points

(For discussion in small groups, write each 'Talking Point' on a separate piece of card.)

1. What makes Crocky and Patch Eye become such good allies?

2. What finally persuades Janet to break her promise? Can you stick up for her and defend what she does?

3. Do you think Crocky was wise to go into hiding? If you'd been there, what advice would you have given him?

Investigations

1. If you could continue the play, what would you want to happen to Crocky when he made his escape on PC Bell's bicycle? Continue the story as far into the future as you want. Crocky's life is now in your hands, so you can give your story a happy or a tragic ending.

2. At the end of the play, Janet watches Crocky make his escape. There's been no time for her to tell Crocky why she broke her promise and gave away his secret.

Imagine that later she decides to write him a letter – wherever he is – explaining her decision.

Write Janet's letter. It ought to begin:

> *Dear Crocky*
> *I heard from Patch Eye that he could get a letter to you so I'm taking a chance and I'm going to try to explain . . .*

She would tell him how the adults persuaded her to say where he was. Would she also ask him to forgive her?

And if Crocky ever took the time to reply, what would he write in his letter to her?

It might be interesting to compare the different letters in a class display.

3. Crocky is on probation for stealing from shops. If he's caught this time he may also have to face a charge of stealing a bicycle.

Write the report that Crocky's social worker would prepare if Crocky was brought before the juvenile court on this new charge.

COUNTY COUNCIL OF EXTON

Social Services Department

Report on: **Michael Crockton**

The report would need to describe his home background; attitude and progress at school; whether or not he had any friends and any other relevant details. You could give these headings in your report: Family, School, Friends, Previous trouble, Recommendations.

4. We often see ourselves differently to the way other people see us. When actors are rehearsing a play they use these differences to help them build a fuller picture of the character they are playing.

   Choose one of the main characters in this play: Crocky, Janet and Patch Eye would be obvious choices. Make a Character Grid like the one below. In the first column, write down what the character says about his or her physical appearance, character and background etc. In the second column, write down what other people say about that person. Check out the differences, and discuss how they could lead to conflicts between your character and other people.

   You'll need to look back through your script to help in your research.

Character's Name:	What the character says about self	What others in play say about that character
Physical Appearance		
Character		
Other things/ Background		

5. Years later, when Janet is an adult, she tells Crocky's story to a new friend.

   Working in pairs, take on the parts of Janet and the friend. What will Janet say about the events of that time? Will she say she's sorry for what happened?

The friend asks a lot of questions. It's a good story and the friend wants to know all the details.

6. There are some strong characters in this play, including some who don't ever appear, like Crocky's grandmother.

Set up a class interview where you can question Crocky and other characters about their part in his story. Volunteers will be needed to take on each character. One way of deciding who takes which character is to do a 'lucky dip'. Put all the characters' names (including those that don't appear, like Gran and Crocky's mother) into a hat. Take it in turns to pick out a character.

You can challenge the characters as well as questioning them. Get them to defend their actions and attitudes. Ask them if you think they acted wisely and whether they would do things any differently now that they know what happened to Crocky. You could also give them advice.

7. Crocky gets into trouble with his father for going to his grandmother's house. His father says, 'You were told not to see her . . . She's not bringing you up. I am.'

What do you think has happened to make the father so angry about Crocky's relationship with his gran?

In pairs, work out a scene which brings the conflict out into the open. You could choose to involve any of the characters . . . and don't forget that Crocky has a mum who we never see! In the argument that follows, give some ideas of the reasons behind this split in family loyalties.

8. Design the front cover illustration for a paperback version of *Real Baddy*, and then write a brief summary of the plot to go on the back cover. Your aim is to make the story look and sound as exciting as possible. You want people to pick up the book and buy it!

9. The stage directions and the speeches give you some idea of the area surrounding Crocky's hiding place. Make an imaginary map of the area. You will get some clues from looking back in the script. You will also have your own imaginary picture of what the area was like.

NORA'S ARK

Nona Shepphard

THE CHARACTERS

The Crew:

Nora Blue, the captain of the ship. Nora is a woman who loves words.
   She has a rich vocabulary. It's a part that needs to be taken by somebody
   who is a very good reader, and who can play it with bags of energy!

Ready, an android

Jenks, the ship's handyman (male)

Nam Yu, the ship's cook (male)

Marly, the mechanic (female)

The Passengers:

Tini Hippolyte, a London girl with a West Indian father and an English
   mother

Billy O'Grady, from Belfast

J.B. (Jumping Bean) Gordon, a black Londoner

Sassie Gordon, J.B.'s sister

Shazia Saleem, an Indian girl from Leeds

Johnathan Shotwell, from Surrey and very 'posh'

Charlotte (Lotty) Morgan, from Wales

About this play

It all takes place on a ship – of sorts! It is, in fact, a ship that's ready to launch
off into space. Its captain is Nora Blue. Her right-hand person is Ready, an
android, whom Nora has made. She called him/her Ready so she/he would be
ready for anything. As indeed Nora herself is. Her cook is called Nam Yu. He's
the finest cook in the world. In charge of washing, cleaning, and sorting is
Jenks – Mr Jenks to you – an old-fashioned gentleman's gentleman who has
fallen on hard times. The engine room is in the very capable hands of Marly

(short for Marlene) the mechanic, who looked after Nora's car for years until the garage owner threw her out for singing too loudly.

Also on the ship are seven young people from all over Britain. When the play opens, the seven are lying asleep. They gradually wake, but they've no idea where they are or what they're doing in this strange place. They start to get to know each other and, little by little, they begin to unscramble the mystery of *Nora's Ark*.

(Nora's ship is a cross between an old-fashioned wooden sailing boat interior, and a high-tech-ultra-modern computerised control room. It is semi-circular in design. Set into the walls are the various control and instrument panels, also washing-machines, an oven, cupboards, waste-disposal chutes, and a long table which pulls out of the wall, so that twelve people can sit and eat.

We can see seven young people standing in seven small cubicles which are set into the walls of the ship. The young people are held in place by metal rings attached to their wrists, feet, chest and necks. Their eyes are closed. There are two sliding doors one on either side, and large double doors in the centre.

One of the side doors slides open, and in sweeps **Nora Blue**, *captain of the ship. She is an eccentrically dressed woman in her sixties. Following her is a person who looks like a man and a woman at the same time. It is* **Ready** – *she/he is an android.*

Nora *takes up position on a small round raised area in the centre, while* **Ready** *stands at a control panel.)*

Nora   Ready, Ready?

Ready   Ready, Captain.

Nora   Oh, I feel so nervous now the moment has come: like the prince must have felt when he woke Sleeping Beauty . . . 'How will she react to being woken up after a hundred years . . . ? Will she like me?'

Ready   They haven't been asleep for a hundred years; only twenty-four hours.

Nora   No, I know that! I was being allegorical . . .

Ready   What's that?

Nora   Allegory means to describe one subject in the disguise of another . . . thus, I was feeling very apprehensive at the thought of waking these young people because I've spent a long time finding them and they mean *so* much to our voyage, and I don't know how they are going to react to finding themselves in a strange place with people they've never met before . . . etcetera, etcetera, so I used the story of the Sleeping Beauty –

Ready OK. I get the picture. Shall we get on?

Nora Do you know, I'm really going to have to put an imprint on your memory valves entitled 'How to appreciate the niceties of English Grammar'.

Ready You're just playing for time because you're nervous.

Nora No, I'm not! . . . Yes I am!

Ready Then I shall take the matter out of your sweaty little hands . . .

Nora You can't do that! I made you! You have to wait for my orders!

Ready Ah, but God gave humans free will . . . allegorically speaking, of course!

Nora Why you – !

Ready Temper, temper!

(**Ready** *presses a button. Lights start to flash on and off in each cubicle. Seven different sorts of music can also be heard. The young people start to wake up.*)

Nora What's that awful racket?

(**Ready** *can't hear her over the noise. She shouts . . .*)

Nora WHAT'S THAT AWFUL RACKET????

Ready Well, it's a little touch of my own, Captain . . . You see, I thought that they'd feel very disorientated, so I'm playing each one their favourite piece of music.

(**Nora** *groans.*)

Nora Well cut it out, I can't hear myself think!

Ready What?

Nora   I said – CUT IT OOUUTTT!!!

Ready   There really is no need to shout.

(She/he has switched the music down.)

Nora   That's better. Now, where was I? OH NO, they're nearly with us . . . I think I'll make myself scarce for a bit.

Ready   Coward!

(They both retreat out of sight. The young people are now coming to, but they can't see each other yet because they are trapped in their cubicles.)

Sassie   Where am I? Where am I?

J.B.   Sassie!

Sassie   J.B.! What's going on? Where are we? Ouch!

J.B.   Dunno!

Sassie   Well don't just stand there – come and help me!

J.B.   Er . . . I can't Sass. I'm a bit tied up at the moment.

Sassie   Oh ha ha!

Johnathan   We appear to be unable to move.

Lotty   Full marks for observation . . .

Johnathan   This is not the time for sarcasm.

Lotty   It's not the time for blomin-stupid-obvious remarks.

Billy   Help! Help!

Lotty   That's more like it – the direct approach –

Shazia   Who's tied us up? Where are we?

Others   Help! HELP!

Tini   Oh shut up the lot of you! Shouting 'help' won't help.

Billy   Why not?

Tini   Because the person – or people – who will hear us shouting, are likely to be the person – or people – who have put us here in the first place.

J.B.   Good thinking, Batwoman . . so what do we do?

Tini   We try to work out why we're here. Do any of you know each other?

J.B.   Sure. That's my sister Sassie over there.

Tini   Hi Sassie! I'm Tini.

Sassie   Hi, Tini . . . My brother J.B. is two along from you.

Tini   And who's next to me?

Billy   Me, I think. My name's Billy.

Tini   Hello, Billy.

Johnathan   Shall I pass round the tea and cucumber sandwiches?

Tini   What's that got to do with anything?

Johnathan   Well, you sound like you're sitting on the lawn having a chat, instead of being in an extremely dangerous situation!

Lotty   Oooh! Tea on the lawn! Bit posh, aren't we?

Johnathan   Oh shut up, I didn't mean –

Tini   Are you Welsh?

Lotty   Yes, I am . . . my name's Charlotte, but everyone calls me Lotty.

Johnathan   Potty Lotty!

Lotty   Oh very witty.

Sassie   What's your name, cucumber?

Johnathan   Johnathan.

Tini   That's six of us.

Shazia   No, seven . . . there's me too . . . I'm Shazia. I'm next to Lotty I think.

Tini   Is there anybody else?

(Silence.)

Tini   So, there's seven of us, and none of us know each other, except Sassie and J.B. Right?

Shazia   What does J.B. stand for?

Sassie   Jumping Bean . . . it's a nickname he got 'cos of the way he dances . . . He's a wicked dancer . . . We do an act; I play and he dances . . .

Johnathan   But surely your parents can't have christened you Jumping Bean?

J.B.   Haven't got any parents.

Tini   Neither have I! Maybe that's the connection.

Lotty   No . . . I've got two . . . worst luck.

Shazia   And me.

Johnathan   Well I've got them too, but I never see them.

Lotty   Lucky you!

Tini   What about Billy?

Billy   My mother brings us up. My Da's away.

Shazia   Are they separated?

Billy   No. My Da's in prison.

Johnathan   What did he do?

Billy   Nothing like you're thinking. He's what they call a political prisoner . . . I live in Belfast.

Lotty   My brother served in Belfast.

Billy   With the British Army?

Lotty   Yes. Sorry.

Johnathan   You don't have to apologise . . . The army should be . . .

J.B.   This is unreal! Here we are . . . in a strange room we don't know where; tied up – we don't know why, and now we're warming up for a political argument! I'm in a loony bin.

Tini   I've been thinking.

J.B.   I'm glad someone has.

Tini And the last thing I remember was going up the hill, past the fish and chip shop, and then seeing this hut – a small brown hut. . . .

Shazia Was it like a garden hut? With green paint round the windows?

Tini That's the one!

Billy I saw that too.

Sassie So did we! D'you remember, J.B.? It was on Waterloo Bridge!

Tini Now we're getting somewhere!

Johnathan It was in the car park, next to the video shop.

Lotty I saw it in the middle of a field!

Tini OK. Now . . . did it have a sign in the window?

Lotty Yes!

Shazia That's right!

Billy It did!

*(They all begin to shout in agreement. **Nora** and **Ready** have been listening to all this. They smile at each other, and make a thumbs up sign.)*

Tini One at a time, one at a time . . . Shazia! You go first . . .

Shazia Well, I was walking home from school along the side of the playing field, and I was feeling really miserable: and I saw the hut like we all did with a sign in the window. It was the sign that made me stop 'cos it said . . . 'FREE CRUISE! COME AND ENJOY THE CRUISE OF A LIFETIME ABSOLUTELY FREE'. I didn't really believe it, but I was feeling so low, that I thought it was worth going to ask . . . so I went in.

Tini Me too. Anyone else?

Johnathan It happened exactly like that.

Lotty And to me too!

Billy I couldn't believe it would be free.

J.B. Well it wasn't, was it? It wasn't free . . . it was a trick.

Johnathan Someone's played a really nasty trick on us.

Tini It must have been that weird old croney sitting at the counter.

*(**Nora** splutters.)*

Shazia She offered me a cup of tea.

Lotty I had a banana milkshake.

J.B. I had a juice, and Sass had coffee.

Billy
Johnathan Coke!

Tini She offered me a lemon Lucozade! It's my favourite.

J.B. Yugh!

Tini Blimey! Drugged and kidnapped! It's like a film . . . It's amazing! Nothing like this has ever happened to me!

Sassie Nor me! Wow!

J.B. It's unreal.

Shazia Are we sure we're awake?

Billy Pinch yourselves everybody.

Johnathan I don't think it's very funny. Do you think they've demanded a ransom? My father'll be furious.

Lotty Does everyone feel all right? No bones broken or anything?

Sassie I feel great.

J.B. Why would anyone want to kidnap us? Sass and me have got no one except each other.

Billy My ma's got nothing . . . no money — nothing. She couldn't give anything.

Tini And I can't see Lambeth Council forking out for me —

Shazia What do you mean?

Tini I live in a home run by the council.

Lotty   Well, my folks could give them a few sheep from off our farm, but not a lot else. I daresay old cucumber sandwich's parents could spare a couple of thousand, eh?

Johnathan   Possibly.

Lotty   Mind you, they'd get you back then wouldn't they? That'd put them off.

Shazia   That wasn't very nice.

Lotty   It wasn't meant to be.

Shazia   My parents will have gone to the police by now . . . they'll be really worried . . .

Tini   But why us? What have we done? What's the connection? I mean we don't even live anywhere near each other – Wales, Ireland, we're from London . . . you're from the North aren't you, Shazia?

Shazia   Leeds. What about you, Johnathan?

Johnathan   I live in Maresfield in Sussex.

Lotty   With a few holiday homes sprinkled about the country, no doubt.

Johnathan   Oh, give it a rest can't you?

Tini   Yeh, shut up, Lotty. We're all in this together. No point fighting amongst ourselves.

Lotty   Don't tell me to shut up. I can choose who I like and who I don't. I didn't ask to be here in the first place.

Shazia   Well, neither did any of us.

*(**Nora** has been listening to all this intently. She speaks at last.)*

Nora   Oh yes you did!

(They all gasp.)

J.B.   Who said that?

Nora   I did.

J.B.   Who's 'I'?

Nora   That weird old croney who was sitting behind the counter, remember?

(She comes into their sightline.)

Tini   Well, you shouldn't have been listening should you?

Nora   And why shouldn't I? It's my ship!

Billy   Are we on a ship? That's great!

Sassie   Oh no – I get seasick . . .

Nora   Well, no – it's not that sort of ship.

Tini   Why have you brought us here?

Nora   Because you asked.

All   We didn't.

Nora   Oh yes you did.

All   Oh no we didn't!

Nora   OH YES YOU –

*(**Ready** coughs and interrupts.)*

Ready   Get to the point, Captain.

Nora   Ah yes . . . sorry . . . I never could resist a good pantomime. Now where was I?

Ready   Why you brought them here. I'm Ready by the way.

Nora   Yes everybody – meet Ready . . . Ready is my creation.

Billy   What do you mean?

Nora   It's quite clear. Ready is an android. I made him/her.

J.B.   That's wicked!

Nora   Oh no, dear boy, it's good. I don't know what I'd do without Ready.

J.B.   That's what I meant –

Lotty   This is a madhouse . . . I'm getting out of here!

Johnathan   Unfortunately you can't, remember?

Nora Oh silly me, I'm sorry, I quite forgot . . . Ready – release!

(**Ready** *presses a button and the restraining rings slide back. The young people are all freed, but they are very stiff.*)

Nora Those bonds were for no sinister purpose, I assure you . . . They were merely to keep you upright. As you can see, space in the ship is very limited, and I didn't want bodies lying around littering the floor while we were trying to get on with our work.

Tini I've been thinking . . .

Nora Good girl!

Tini About what I was thinking just before I saw your hut.

Nora And what was that?

Tini I'd run out of Stoneybrook – that's the name of the home – and I wasn't going to go back . . . I hate it there and I felt really low, and I thought I'm sick to death of this lousy situation. I wish something'd happen so I could get out. And then I saw the hut with the sign in the window and I thought – that's magic! It was like the answer to a wish –

Ready Yes, Cinderella, you shall go to the Ball!

Nora Exactly so! How I love pantomimes.

Tini So, is that what you meant by saying we asked to come here?

Nora Every single one of you were, for very different reasons, at the end of your tethers! You were all sending out very strong *Help and Rescue* signals over the emotional airwaves. I picked them up and appeared accordingly. I'm very good at ESP, aren't I, Ready?

Ready Extremely perceptive, captain.

Nora You all wanted to get out, didn't you? Well, didn't you?

(*They all nod and reply yes.*)

Nora Well, here you all are . . . OUT! Now, down to practicalities.

Billy Are we really going on a cruise?

Nora   We most certainly are!

Sassie   And it's free?

Nora   Of course!

J.B.   So it won't cost us nothing?

Nora   You won't get anything for nothing in this life, young man; you get out what you put in. I shall expect you to work your passage.

Lotty   How long are we going for?

Nora   I'll explain all that later.

Shazia   But what about our parents?

Nora   What about them?

Shazia   Won't they be worried?

Nora   Since when has that been a concern of yours?

Shazia   Well . . .

Nora   Exactly!

Johnathan   Where are we going to?

Nora   If you'll all just stop asking these infernal questions . . . I'll let you know. Ready, summon the crew!

Ready   I've already done that, Captain. Here they are!

(The other door slides open and a woman and two men come in; they line up in front of the young people.)

Nora   Crew – Atten . . . SHUN! Introduce yourselves.

Ready   You already know me . . . I'm called Ready . . .

Nora   I called her that so he'd be ready for anything.

Ready   And I'm Nora's assistant.

Nora   My right handroid!

(The crew groan.)

Nora   All right, all right . . . next!

Marly I'm Marlene, but you can call me Marly, and I'm in charge of the engine room.

Nora This woman is a genius with anything from changing a plug to interfacing the most advanced computers. We built the ship together. Next!

Jenks My name is Mr Jenkins, but you may call me Mr Jenks.

Nora A real old gentleman's gentleman. We met in a bar.

Jenks I'm in charge of washing, cleaning, tidying, sorting and keeping the ship shipshape.

Nora And last but not least – this is –

Nam Yu Nam Yu. I cook.

Nora The finest cook in the world!

Ready Aren't we forgetting something, captain?

Nora What?

Marly Our Captain . . . Nora Blue!

(*The crew applaud.*)

Lotty They're a bunch of maniacs this lot!

Sassie Ssshh.

Nora Our ship is called *Nora's Ark*.

Ready This is a biblical reference to –

Nora Steady, Ready – let's see if any of them know. Anyone know anything about a similar sounding ship?

J.B. You mean Noah's Ark, don't you?

(*Nora nods.*)

Sassie God said to this geyser, Noah, that he was going to send a flood to destroy the land, but because Noah had been so good, he was giving him this advance warning so he'd be able to save himself and his family.

50 **Shazia** How do you know all that?

Sassie Our Mum and Dad were very churchy. Baptists they were, and we used to have to go every Sunday, didn't we J.B.? And to Sunday school too. J.B. quite liked it . . . I thought it was terrible.

Billy And he took all the animals too, male and female, by twos . . .

Lotty And the flood came and it rained for about a year, and then . . .

Billy No, it wasn't that long!

Lotty It stopped!

J.B. And they sent out birds, and when the dove came back with a bit of branch in its beak, Noah knew that the world had dried off, so he and his family and all the animals, got off the Ark and started again.

Billy And we're all descended from them!

Nora I'm sorry you were left out of that Bible memory test, Shazia dear; I'm sure there must be similar destruction stories in the Koran . . . Ready, remind me to look.

Ready Yes, Captain.

Johnathan So, Nora, God came to you and told you that the earth was going to be destroyed by a flood?

Nora There is no need to be facetious, young man. Is that what they taught you in that very expensive public school of yours? To make fun of your elders?

Ready The captain is using allegory . . . in describing the earth being destroyed by a flood, she is really describing the imminent destruction of the earth, as she sees it, by man.

Nora Horrible little species we are! Vainglorious, arrogant, selfish and boastful! Chopping down forests that have been there for millions of years! Tearing holes in the sky!

Ready The captain is of course referring to the destruction of the world's rainforests . . . and to the hole in the ozone layer caused by CFCs . . . and to the so-called Greenhouse effect which . . .

Nora (*interrupting*) Killing off millions of animals for money!

Ready Five hundred animal species have now become extinct. And many more are in grave danger of becoming so . . . With the extinction of the great whale species, would come the destruction of the precious ecosystems that exist in the world's oceans.

Jenks And might I add, Ma'am, that if the trees do not fall to the axe, and the whales to the exploding harpoon, then they will die anyway, as victims to the toxic wastes which are even now polluting the deepest oceans.

Nora Well put, Jenks.

Nam Yu Food! Half the world too fat! Too much food – too much red meat! Cattle eating grain that would feed other half of the world! One half of world no food! Other half of world butter mountains . . . lakes of wine! One half of world dies of hunger and thirst! Stupid!

Nora I couldn't agree more, Nam Yu.

Marly And if you're still alive after all that, watch out! There's still the machines of war. We don't pour money into machines that will preserve and cure and keep us healthy do we! Oh no; we want to blow ourselves up and make this earth a wasteland.

Ready The countries of the earth have stockpiled enough weapons to destroy the planet hundreds of times over.

Nora All in all, we're making of our beautiful world a rubbish heap, and the wastes will rise up like a flood and choke us.

Tini Blimey . . . you're cheerful, you lot, aren't you?

Nora Of course we're cheerful! But it pays to look around you, keep your wits about you and your eyes open. Got to get problems into perspective!

Johnathan So we're going on a cruise to take our minds off it all?

Nora No. We're going on a cruise to take us *out* of it all.

Ready This is a cruise into space.

Kids What?

Nora I promised you the cruise of a lifetime and that's what you're going to get!

Billy Wow!

Nora This cruise takes you on a drive round the stars, a quick stop off at the moon, a stroll around the rings of Saturn and will end up at a small planet of my acquaintance . . . which I have named Ararat, for obvious reasons!

Shazia What reasons?

J.B. Mount Ararat was where Noah ended up.

Shazia Oh.

Nora Now . . . lift off will be in two hours, and we have a lot of work to do before then.

J.B. Hurray!

Nora So, I am assigning jobs for each of you . . .

(They groan.)

Nora Shazia, you will work with Jenks. Johnathan and J.B., I've put you with Nam Yu. Billy goes with Marly, Lotty and Sassie are with Ready . . . and Tini —

Tini Yeh?

Nora You can come with me.

Tini All right!

Nora Work hard and be good everyone! See you later.

*(They all split up into their respective groups, and go off to different parts of the ship. **Shazia** stays with **Jenks**.)*

Shazia Right Mr Jenks, here I am! What do we do?

Jenks Well, Miss Shazia, we get this table down ready for our dinner, and plates and glasses and knives and forks: and we polish the lot, and then lay the table.

Shazia Right . . . what with?

Jenks Here's a cloth, Miss Shazia.

(They start to work.)

Shazia You don't need to call me Miss Shazia, Mr Jenks . . . just Shazia will do.

Jenks Oh, I couldn't do that, Miss. I can't break the habits of a lifetime . . . I'm too old to change now.

Shazia So, do you think when people get older, they can never change their minds?

Jenks Oh, they can change their *minds*, Miss, I've done a lot of thinking and changing since I met the captain but your *habits* . . . your *customs* . . . they're more difficult . . . You've got used to them . . . grown into them, so to speak. They make you feel secure, comfortable, they're sort of who you are.

Shazia Mmnn.

Jenks Did you have a particular reason for asking, Miss?

Shazia No . . . well . . . yes. It's my parents really.

Jenks Don't you see eye to eye then, Miss?

Shazia That's putting it mildly . . . they won't let me do anything! It's like a prison! Girls have to wear traditional clothes; keep quiet; look sweet; be in early; stay at home; and learn to cook, clean and keep house, so as to be ready for the husband my parents are going to arrange for me. They've advertised in the papers back in India. Can you believe it?

Jenks I can, Miss; but I can't see you being happy with that.

Shazia I'm not . . . I hate it. I sneak out with a change of clothes and make up in a plastic bag and go out with my friends . . . Last night – or whenever it was . . . I stayed out all night.

Jenks Oh dear. What happened?

Shazia My father shouted and raged and said I wasn't to leave the house for a month. My mother cried a lot.

Jenks Understandable. They must have been very worried.

Shazia I know that but – it's not fair! I don't do anything awful . . . I just want to have a good time . . . I do my studies . . . I want to go to university. Course, I haven't told them that, they'd probably forbid me to go. Girls are for marriage, not careers.

Jenks   They'd probably be very proud, if they knew.

Shazia   What you were saying about customs and things . . . It's not that I don't value and respect our culture . . . I do, and I know why they want to preserve it . . . and keep it alive . . .

Jenks   But you want to make your own sense out of things.

Shazia   Yes. I don't know India. I've never even been there . . . I was born in Leeds. I'm British. And Indian. I can be both . . . have the best of two worlds! What's the problem?

Jenks   Maybe the problem's smaller than you think, Miss.

Shazia   You don't know my father.

Jenks   Have you spoken to them? Like you've been speaking to me, I mean?

Shazia   Ha! Fat chance. They wouldn't listen.

Jenks   They might.

Shazia   They wouldn't. I know them.

Jenks   So never the twain shall meet.

Shazia   What?

Jenks   Nothing, Miss. Just seems a shame that's all.

*(They carry on preparing the table for dinner. Meanwhile **Nam Yu**, **J.B.** and **Johnathan** have been chopping a mountain of vegetables. They continue as they speak.)*

J.B.   Where are the hamburgers, then?

Nam Yu   On my table no hamburgers. Understand? Junk! Junk food! Full of additives, full of –

J.B.   All right, all right, keep your hair on. It was only a joke. J.B. will eat healthy. OK?

Nam Yu   OK. You. Very good at this. You make good cook.

Johnathan   Thank you.

Nam Yu   You. Hopeless. Horrible cook.

J.B.   Thank you.

Nam Yu   In my family, art passed down from father to son, father to son . . . six generations top-class cooks. Same with you?

Johnathan   I'm afraid not, no. My father's a property developer.

J.B.   Well, I haven't got anywhere to live . . . maybe he could develop me a property.

Johnathan   Oh good God . . . he doesn't build anything so useful as housing . . . Not enough profits in it, dear boy. Office space – that's where the money is.

Nam Yu   He very rich?

Johnathan   Stinking, filthy rich, you might say.

J.B.   Lucky you!

Nam Yu   So, you be property tycoon, like your father?

Johnathan   Not if I can help it.

J.B.   Still, if he's that rich, you won't have to do anything . . . just jet around the world.

Johnathan   That wouldn't do for my father . . . oh dearie me, no. He's a self-made man. Graft . . . that's what he believes in. A man's not a man unless he works a sixteen-hour day!

J.B.   Well, it did a lot for him. Don't knock it.

Nam Yu   What do *you* want to do?

Johnathan   There's only one thing I really want to do, but I won't be allowed to do it.

J.B.   What's that?

Johnathan   I'm not telling you – you'll laugh!

Nam Yu   No laugh.

Johnathan   You will.

J.B.   We won't. We promise, don't we, Nam Yu? Scouts honour.

Johnathan   I want to be a dancer.

(J.B. bursts out laughing.)

Johnathan   You see? And you promised!

J.B.   I'm not laughing at you. I'm just laughing at the big deal you're making out of it. I dance . . . I dance all the time . . . me and Sass make money out of it. On the streets in Covent Garden, in London. We can make a good few bob!

Johnathan   I don't mean that sort of dancing . . . I mean classical dancing . . . ballet.

Nam Yu   Good. You do it.

Johnathan   Oh sure. You can imagine what my father thinks about a son of his being a ballet dancer . . . he'd go spare.

J.B.   Let him. I think it's great . . . you come down to Covent Garden and do some classes . . . There's plenty of studios teach ballet.

Johnathan   Are there?

J.B.   Where have you been living? Course there are – I used to do a few myself.

Johnathan   You did ballet?

(J.B. puts on a jokey accent: he mimics a slave talking to his master.)

J.B.   Sure. Us young black boys don't just do break dancing and hip hop, massah sir! Tho' I know you white dudes think it's all we good fo'!

Johnathan   I'm sorry! I was making assumptions.

J.B.   You sure were.

Johnathan   If . . . if . . . I were to come and do some classes, would you come with me?

J.B.   What for . . . to hold your hand?

Johnathan   Of course. I'm terrified! Well . . . would you come?

J.B.   Don't know.

Johnathan   Scared I'm better than you?

J.B.   Nobody's better than me!

Johnathan Well then?

J.B. I've no time.

Nam Yu He no money.

Johnathan I've got money, loads of money . . . I'll pay for us both!

J.B. Don't be stupid! I don't want your money. I can look after myself.

Johnathan I'm sure you can. But if you can't afford the classes, I could . . .

J.B. Look, shut up! Just *you* do some classes . . . and you never know . . . I might win the pools and buy us a school!

(*They go on working. Meanwhile **Marly** and **Billy** have been taking the oven apart.*)

Marly Oh now I see what's wrong! We haven't been able to use this in weeks. I'll fix it, and put it back together again.

Billy What will I do?

Marly You just sit down there and relax . . .

Billy I can help you.

Marly You can't . . . it's a one person job, this. Take the weight off your feet.

(***Billy** sits down. There is a comfortable silence for some time.*)

Marly What're you thinking about?

Billy Nothing.

Marly It's good to do that, eh?

Billy It's brilliant.

Marly Don't get much time to yourself?

Billy No . . . none.

Marly Share your bedroom?

Billy My ma and my two sisters sleep in one room and me and our Shaun and Andy sleep in the other.

Marly   You the oldest?

Billy   Aye.

Marly   And your mum's on her own . . . so you help look after the family?

Billy   Have to . . . there's no one else . . . and my ma goes out to work.

Marly   And so do you?

Billy   In the mornings before school, and on a Saturday.

Marly   So between that and school and homework and looking after the littler ones and helping keep house, you don't have much time for play?

Billy   My ma sends me out to play football in the flats . . . whenever she can . . . but she gets tired.

Marly   And so do you.

Billy   Aye.

Marly   And recently, you've been so tired, you were thinking of running away?

Billy   How did you know?

Marly   I had a life like that when I was young.

Billy   I won't run away though.

Marly   Course not. You love your Mum.

Billy   Aye. And all the rest of them! But, I'll just sit here for a bit more, and then I'd better be getting back.

Marly   To Belfast?

Billy   Yes.

Marly   Well then, you carry on . . .

(There is silence again.
*Meanwhile, in another part of the ship, **Lotty** and **Sassie** have been working with **Ready**. He is showing them a picture on the screen. **Lotty** shrieks.)*

Lotty   Oh, you can't be serious! That's not it, is it?

Ready It most certainly is . . . That is Ararat, our destination planet . . . isn't it beautiful?

Sassie It's gorgeous!

Lotty Beautiful? Gorgeous? It's horrible! It's disgusting!

Sassie But it's so colourful. Look at those oranges and reds . . . and the pink sky.

Lotty What are those things?

Ready That's a flock of Grazelings . . . similar to your cows or sheep, I think.

Lotty They're not a bit like sheep, and grass is supposed to be green . . . not orange. And water's supposed to be blue not . . . not . . . that vile colour.

Sassie Well, I think it looks lovely and I can't wait to see it.

Lotty Well, I'm going to give it a miss!

Sassie There's no pleasing you is there? You've just spent the last half-hour moaning about where you live and how small it is and how boring it is and how you're sick of looking at grass, grass, grass and sheep, sheep, sheep, and about how you're sick of waking up to the same old view from your bedroom window, and how boring your parents are and why don't they live in the city instead of the boring old country that's like a morgue. Well, I wish I had my parents alive, and I wish I had a bedroom, and a home and a village, and I didn't have to live on the streets in the city you think's so exciting, and I wish J.B. could go to dance school like he wants and . . . and I can't have any of that! But I *can* go on this cruise, and see this planet, and I'm going to love it and so are you, so be quiet and shut up!

Lotty Oh all right. Point taken.

Sassie About time . . . how long will we stay on Ararat, Ready?

Ready Stay? What do you mean?

Lotty Well, when are we going to come back?

Ready We're not coming back.

Sassie We're not coming back?

Lotty What?

Ready The captain has no intention of coming back. She thinks the earth's a lost cause. We shall live on Ararat and start a new world.

Lotty Oh come on – be serious!

Ready I am serious. We are not coming back.

Sassie Never ever?

Ready Not as far as I know.

Lotty Let me get this straight . . . She wants us to live on that? For ever?

Ready Of course. Didn't you know?

Lotty Of course I didn't know. I don't want to live on that for ever. It's bad enough for a visit.

Sassie Well, I'm game! Anything's got to be better than sleeping out on the streets.

Lotty Well, I'm not! I've got to get out of here.

Ready You can't do that either. There must be no leak of information about the ship's existence, or its departure or destination. Surely you must see that?

Lotty So we're prisoners?

Ready You wanted to come, remember?

Lotty But I didn't bargain for this! Come on Sassie, quick! Let's go and find the others.

(They run off, followed by **Ready.** **Nora** *and* **Tini** *come on the opposite side. They have been doing a tour of the ship.)*

Nora So there you are, my dear, now you have seen everything . . . what do you think of her?

Tini I think she's fantastic.

Nora And you think you can cope with being second in command?

Tini Why did you choose me?

Nora Because, you are definitely captain material . . . you have great qualities of leadership my dear. Did nobody ever tell you that before?

Tini Yeh . . .

Nora Well, there you are.

Tini But not in the way you think.

Nora How then?

Tini Well, I was part of . . . the leader of a gang at the home and . . . well . . .

Nora This gang wasn't a constructive part of community life?

Tini You could put it like that.

Nora In fact, this gang was very destructive?

Tini Yeh. The superintendent said I could choose . . . either I could put my energies to good use, train as a staff member and become what she called a 'responsible member of society' – Yuch!

Nora Or?

Tini Or . . . they'd throw me out! I'm turned sixteen, see.

Nora And?

Tini I got thrown out . . . yesterday . . . or whenever it was . . . She said much as it hurt her to do it – very likely! – she said she had the other kids to consider and I was a very bad influence on the younger ones.

Nora And were you?

Tini Well, she obviously thought so. And what she says, goes. It doesn't matter what I think.

Nora And what do you think?

Tini I think . . . a lot of the kids like me. They sort of look up to me, and there isn't enough for them to do there . . . games and sport and discos and stuff . . . so they get miserable. A lot of them miss their mums and dads or families if they've got them . . . They're funny places to live in – kids' homes.

Nora　And you should know. Your mother left you seven years ago, didn't she?

Tini　That's right! How did you know?

Nora　ESP, my dear. Extra sensory perception! Did you never think of using all this knowledge and experience?

Tini　What me? I'm not clever, I haven't got those things.

Nora　That's not what I perceive, Tini. You could've put your knowledge and experience to good use. The superintendent clearly thought a lot of you . . . and so did the other children . . . and you're obviously fond of them . . . so why didn't you —

(We hear shouts from off.)

Kids　Tini! Tini! Where are you?

Tini　I'm in here.

(The others all rush in.)

Nora　What a noise . . . what on earth's the matter?

Lotty　We've got to talk to Tini.

Nora　Well, here she is! Talk!

Lotty　Could we . . . er . . . talk to Tini on her own?

Nora　Ah! You mean you want me to make myself scarce?

Billy　That's right . . . sorry.

Nora　Anything you say, my dears.

(She is about to go.)

Tini　No, Nora, don't go.

*(**Nora** stays.)*

Tini　You can say what you have to say in front of her.

Lotty　No, we can't.

Nora　This sounds ominous!

Tini　Oh come on, what is it?

Lotty   She has to go.

Tini   Why? I trust her . . . she's all right.

Lotty   You won't when you hear what we've got to say. Come on,
Tini . . . you're one of us.

Tini   Why am I one of you? I've never met you before . . . I've
spent time with Nora . . . she knows me better than you do.
What's the matter?

Billy   We're not coming back!

Tini   What?

Lotty   From this planet we're going to! We're not coming back
. . . and the doors are locked so we can't leave the ship 'cos she
doesn't want anyone to know about it.

Billy   We're taking off soon –

Shazia   And we're never coming back!

Johnathan   Never!

Sassie   We're going to make a new life on Ararat and have homes
there, and live there forever!

J.B.   I don't know why you're looking so pleased, Sass. You look
like you want to go.

Sassie   Well, so I do.

(*Tini has been looking at* **Nora**.)

Tini   Is this true?

Nora   Not entirely.

Tini   There you are!

Nora   It is true that we will not be coming back to earth.

Lotty   There *you* ARE!

Nora   But it is not true that you will not be allowed to leave. As if
I should want to spend the rest of my days with a bunch of
people who didn't want to be there! The very idea! No, I have
clearly been mistaken . . . I thought all of you had had enough
of your lives on Earth . . . at least those were the signals you

were sending out. But obviously not! I shall give you five minutes, for time is getting short. Those that want to go, may go freely, on the condition that they breathe no word to anyone about the existence of this ship and its crew. Those that want to partake in the 'Cruise of a Lifetime' will be more than welcome. You must choose.

(The young people are silent as they think about what to do. The rest of the crew come in and watch.
Shazia *goes over to* **Jenks.***)*

Shazia   What do you think I ought to do, Mr Jenks?

Jenks   Oh, that's not for me to say, Miss Shazia.

Shazia   I think I know what you think.

Jenks   It's what *you* think that counts.

Shazia   And I think . . . I'd better go home and do some talking.

Jenks   Just so, Miss.

(**Nam Yu** *goes up to* **Johnathan.***)*

Nam Yu   You go back to dance?

Johnathan   Well, I'm going to go back and try.

(**Nam Yu** *looks over to where* **J.B.** *and* **Sassie** *are sitting apart.)*

Nam Yu   You get your father to build them a house?

Johnathan   I don't know if they'll be coming back yet. I hope J.B. does. If I turn out to be a lousy dancer, maybe I should take over the old firm, and start building something useful.

Nam Yu   Maybe . . .

(**J.B.** *and* **Sassie** *look at each other.)*

Sassie   You want to go back, don't you?

J.B.   Yeh. And you don't?

Sassie   No. Why do you? What is there here?

J.B.   Well, I wouldn't say this to anyone but you, Sass; but, when old Nora was doing her speech like a prophet of Doom about pollution and all that . . . I got angry! I wanted to do something about it. I like London. I want it to stick around.

Sassie   What can we do . . . we live among the mess.

J.B.   So who better than us to know what we're up against?

Sassie   Mum and Dad always wanted us to see Trinidad.

J.B.   And we can't do that if we're out amongst the stars can we?

Sassie   I could go, and you could stay.

J.B.   No! I'll come if you really want to go.

Sassie   So who'll save the world if you do go?

J.B.   Don't laugh at me, sister, I'm serious.

Sassie   I know.

(*Marly goes up to where **Billy** is sitting.*)

Marly   You don't look as if you're struggling to make up your mind.

Billy   I'm not . . . there's enough struggles at home. I'm just making the most of these last minutes of peace and quiet.

(*Lotty stands with **Ready**.*)

Lotty   Will you do something for me?

Ready   Of course.

Lotty ˙ Send me back a picture of you milking those creatures of yours!

Ready   Of course I will. Their milk's delicious. It's green.

Lotty   Green like my home . . . I'm glad something there is!

(*Tini goes up to **Nora**.*)

Tini   I'm going back, Nora.

Nora   That's my girl!

Tini   You don't mind?

Nora   Well, I'll miss your company, of course, but you have unfinished business you need to attend to. I expect great things from you, my girl. I want you running the country at the very least.

Tini   Well, let me start by seeing if I can run my own life first!

Nora   You've already started, my dear.

(She claps her hands.)

Nora   Well, time's up, everyone! Hands up those who are staying.

(Nobody raises their hands.)

Nora   Not even you, Sassie?

Sassie   No, I'd love to come but . . . I couldn't bear not to see my brother's ugly face again!

J.B.   Sassie, you're brilliant!

Sassie   Does it take all this to make you realise that?

Johnathan   I'm really pleased you're coming back, J.B.

Nora   I think we all deserve a celebratory drink! Ready, Ready?

*(**Ready** brings out a drinks tray with all their favourite drinks on it.)*

Ready   All ready, Captain.

Tini   Lemon Lucozade! My favourite!

Kids   Yugh!

Nora   Here's to you all! May you have long and happy lives!

Lotty   Here's to *you* all, and your life on Ararat! And I want you to all make sure there's an Earth still here and looking good . . . if ever we should want to visit!

All   Cheers!

*(Everybody drinks. The young people make their 'goodbyes' and leave one by one. The doors shut. **Nora** and her crew are left.)*

Nora   Well, what are you all standing around like stuffed lemons for? We've got work to do! Action stations everyone!

Crew   Yes, Captain.

*(They scatter leaving **Nora** and **Ready**.)*

Nora Well, they were a nice bunch weren't they, Ready?

Ready Very nice indeed, Captain.

Nora I wonder what the next lot are going to be like?

Ready I'm picking up a Help and Rescue, Captain!

Nora Where from?

Ready Somewhere called Macclesfield, Captain – in Cheshire.

Nora Ah, dear Cheshire! Ready, Ready?

(**Ready** *nods.*)

Talking Points

(*For discussion in small groups, write each 'Talking Point' on a separate piece of card.*)

1. How has Nora gathered her group together?

Why did she trick them?

2. Are the kids making a fuss over nothing about their problems?

What advice would you give each one?

3. Is Nora overdoing the gloomy future for planet Earth?

Does Nora have any solutions to planet Earth's problems?

Investigations

1. The planet Ararat does not exist, but Nora wants the young people to believe that it does. She describes it in glowing detail.

Look back through the script (particularly page 60) to find out all you can about the planet. Then, once you've done your research and collected your information, use it to compile *A Tourist Guide to Ararat*.
Remember that guide books often contain a lot of illustrations: include as many as you can.

If you prefer, you could put together a more honest guide book, mentioning the drawbacks of life on Ararat as well as the attractions.

2. **'CHILDREN KIDNAPPED BY GARDEN SHED!'**
That's the headline in this week's local paper. Write the story that goes with the headline.

3. When the young people return from Nora's Ark, the national press has taken up the story. So have the radio and television companies. Set up a press conference at which the main characters are interviewed about their experiences. The conference might be controlled by a local police inspector (played by your teacher?).

Use your knowledge of the character to answer as realistically and convincingly as possible.

The rest of the class become members of the press, television reporters, radio journalists etc. Identify who you are, and what paper/TV programme you come from before putting your question.

4. Nora keeps **Datafiles** of all her clients. At the end of the play, Nora goes off to Macclesfield on another 'Help and Rescue' call. As a class, put together the **Datafiles** which record full details of Nora's clients for this next mission. Nora uses a form like this:

NORA'S ARK	DATAFILE
Name of Client	
Address	
Age	
Reason they want to escape this planet	
Suggestions for helping the client cope with their problem	

Everyone prepare one **Datafile**.

5. Get into small groups. Choose one of the young characters in the play, or one of those on your class **Datafiles**. Work out the scene that takes place when that person returns home.

   You'll need to decide who plays the young person and who else — family members, friends? — will be present when he or she returns.

   Present your scenes to the class. After each one, discuss whether you think the central character is going to regret going back. Will they be able to carry through their new approach to their problem? Does it seem as if the other members of their family — or their friends — will need re-educating too? Do you think they could do with a visit from Nora?

6. Make a **Missing Person** poster for one of the young people in the play. The poster will include a 'photograph' (which could be either a drawing or a picture from a magazine). With the 'photograph', you'll also need to provide: a detailed description of the person; information as to when and where they were last seen; and an address for informants to contact.

7. Design the set for a stage production of *Nora's Ark*. You'll need not only the main deck of Nora's ship, but also several acting areas for the short scenes in the second part of the play (e.g. pages 53, 55, 58). How realistic do you want the set to be?

   From outside, the ship is supposed to look like a garden shed. How would you reflect this inside?

   Perhaps you could develop the design sketch into a scale model?

JACKS AND KINGS

Maria Oshodi

THE CHARACTERS

Drew (Andrew) King, aged 13, of mixed race. His parents are divorced
Clive King, Drew's father. He is black and is now married to . . .
Gill King, who is white
Holly King, daughter of Clive and Gill, of mixed race

May Jacks, Drew's mother. She is white and is now married to . . .
Eddie Jacks, who is also white, and has a white son from a previous
  marriage . . .
Mikey Jacks, Drew's stepbrother, who is white

Tina King   ⎫ Drew's twin sisters, aged 12,
Dawn King   ⎭ also of mixed race

In the neighbourhood are:
Bobby Moss, who is black
Mrs Moss
Rita, a shop assistant
The vicar

There are a few very small speaking parts for Bobby Moss's friends

About this play

Drew has a black father and a white mother. They're divorced, so Drew and
his sisters live with his mother and her new husband. After a family
argument, Drew decides to leave. He says that his new father never takes
his side and that's because his new dad is white. Drew wants to be with his
real father. He's black and that's what Drew considers himself to be. So, he
chooses to be loyal to one parent at the expense of the other. But is he
being loyal for the right reasons or is he just fooling himself?

71

SCENE 1

*(A council estate in the city. **Drew** is coming home from school. As he turns the corner by the garages, he is met by his younger sisters, **Dawn** and **Tina**, and his half-brother, **Mikey**. They are shouting and screaming because they're being chased by **Bobby Moss** and his friends. The girls and **Mikey** take cover behind **Drew** and yell at **Bobby**.)*

Dawn   We don't have to if we don't want to!

Tina   You can't make us!

Bobby   Yes you do right, 'cos I said so!

Drew   What's going on?

*(**Mikey** calls to **Bobby**.)*

Mikey   And what about Drew?

Bobby   He's gotta as well.

Drew   Gotta what?

Dawn   We were all gonna have a game of run-outs Drew, but Bobby goes 'we can't play till we say we're black.'

Bobby   Yeah, 'cos it's a black game of run-outs.

Drew   Why black?

Bobby   'Cos black is faster, stronger, badder. You playing Drew?

Drew   Only if they can.

*(**Drew** points at his sisters and **Mikey**.)*

Bobby   He can't 'cos he ain't black, and those two . . . *(Pointing at **Tina** and **Dawn**.)* They've gotta choose, either black or white.

Drew   I ain't choosing either.

Bobby   If you don't choose black, then you're dirty white and you can't play neither.

Mikey   We don't care. We'll play pat ball instead.

Bobby   Not against the garages you won't. It's only us hanging out here from now on.

Tina   That's what he thinks doesn't he, Drew?

Bobby Shut your mouth, Nescafé.

Bobby's friends Nescafé . . . Nescafé . . . Nescafé . . .

(They fall about laughing.)

Bobby When are you making your next coffee advert?

(He laughs with his friends.)

Drew You shut your mouth, right!

Bobby You think you can batter the black brother? Just try it.

Tina Go on Drew!

Dawn Yeah, go on Drew!

*(**Bobby** and **Drew** begin to fight.)*

Mikey Go on!

(The rest circle them, yelling them on.)

SCENE 2

*(An hour later, in the kitchen of the Jacks's flat. **May Jacks** comes home from work. **Mikey** is there watching television.)*

May Hiya, tribe! Are you all ready for tea?

Kids *(from all over the flat)* Yeah!

May It's curried meat balls and jacket spuds.

*(A cheer goes up from several rooms. **Dawn** wanders through the kitchen.)*

Dawn Mum, you know Bobby Moss at number five?

May I do.

Dawn Drew beat him up just now, 'cos he was picking on us.

*(**Tina** bursts in.)*

Tina It's five o'clock! I wanna watch the charts

(She moves to the set and switches channels.)

Mikey What d'you think you're doing? Turn it back!

Tina   Hush up you mouth, Mikey. You've been watching it. It's my turn now. Oh Mum, I've just seen Bobby Moss's mum. She's coming to see you.

Mikey   I was watching it first, Tina.

(*Dawn* wanders in again.)

Dawn   Mikey, Drew's moving your fishing set.

Mikey   No, he ain't.

(He runs out. As he does, there is a knock on the front door.)

Tina   That's probably Bobby Moss's mum.

May   Tell her I'm coming out to see her.

(*Dawn* goes to open the front door. She calls back to her mother.)

Dawn   It's my friend Joanne. Where are my skates, Mum? I wanna go out.

(*May* goes to the doorway and calls into the hall.)

May   Don't go far! I don't want to lose my voice calling you over the balcony when the food is ready. Your skates are in the cupboard.

Dawn   Thanks! See you!

(*Dawn* leaves the house to go roller skating.)

May   Has anyone seen the dog's bowl?

Tina   Yeah, Mikey took it to mix some glue in.

(*Mikey* and *Drew* start shouting in their bedroom. They can be heard in the kitchen.)

Mikey   Don't chuck my stuff!

Drew   I can't get under my bed to get my bike chain, or pump, or nothing.

May   There they go again.

Mikey   What am I meant to do with it, then?

Drew   Look; that's the middle of the room. Get it on your side!

Tina   Shut up, you two. I can't hear the telly!

Mikey   I've got more stuff than you. I should have more room.

(*Drew comes into the kitchen, followed by* *Mikey*.)

Drew   Tough! You shouldn't have more stuff then.

Mikey   Tough, 'cos I have.

May   Come on you two, stop fighting over nothing.

(*The boys scowl at each other. There is a bang on the kitchen door.* *Mrs Jacks* *goes to open it.* *Mrs Moss* *is outside. She pushes her way into the kitchen, holding a torn and dirty jacket.*)

Mrs Moss   I want to have a word with you!

May   Do you?

Mrs Moss   Yes, I do. That boy of yours has kicked my Bobby and ripped his jacket. Look at it now. It looks like something he found on a rubbish tip. Who would believe it cost £75?

May   That's what comes from dressing your kids in designer clothes.

Mrs Moss   No, it comes from when they have to mix with kids who behave like animals. Still, I'm not surprised Drew is like a delinquent, coming from a family where's there's no real dad and all the kids are different colours.

May   If you've finished, then I'll tell you something about animals and delinquents. (*She turns to* *Drew*.) Tell her why you did what you did to Bobby.

Drew   'Cos he kept calling me and Tina and Dawn names.

Mrs Moss   My Bobby wouldn't do that. What sort of names?

(*Dawn* *suddenly bursts into the kitchen with a whimpering dog.*)

Dawn   Mum look! We found Jay Jay with his mouth stuck together.

Drew   Tell her what Bobby was calling us Dawn.

Dawn   Nescafé.

Mrs Moss   Nescafé?

Tina 'Cos he was trying to get us to say we're black and join his gang, and we said 'no.'

May Mikey, look at the dog. He's gone and eaten that glue you mixed up in his bowl. You could have killed him. You're going to have to take him to the vet and pay for the bill out of your pocket money.

Mikey Oh please, May! I'm meant to go fishing with that money on Saturday. It ain't fair!

May Look at poor Jay Jay. Is that fair?

(*Eddie opens the door and comes into the kitchen.*)

Eddie Hello, what's going on in here?

(*Everyone starts to talk at once.*)

Eddie Hold on, I've only got one pair of ears! Now lets start with you, Mrs Moss isn't it?

Mrs Moss Your son . . . her son . . . well, anyway, him there, Drew . . . look, look what he's done to my Bobby's jacket. He's ripped the pocket clean off.

Eddie Oh dear, I'm very sorry.

May Don't apologise until you've heard Drew's side.

Eddie Hold on May! Whatever happened, Drew does not go around ripping up other people's clothes.

Dawn Drew only done it 'cos Bobby called us Nescafé.

Eddie What on earth does that mean?

May The nasty little thing's talking about their colour isn't he? He's saying it's like coffee.

Eddie Is that all! Well, remember Drew, names can never hurt you, but ripped pockets can . . . because it's going to cost you your pocket money to get it mended.

Mrs Moss Sounds fine by me.

Eddie Why is Jay Jay making that noise?

May Mikey mixed up some glue in his bowl and he ate it. Now he can't open his mouth. I think it's up to Mikey to take him to the vet.

Eddie *(putting his hand in his pocket)*   Too right. Here you are Mikey, take this tenner to pay the bill.

*(**Mikey** takes the money and starts to leave with the dog but before he gets to the door **Drew** pushes him out of the way and runs out of the flat first, shouting.)*

Drew   You lot make me sick!

Dawn   Drew, where are you going?!

May   Come back! What about your dinner?

*(**Mrs Moss** also starts to leave.)*

Mrs Moss   He's just a little tearaway, you see.

Eddie   Come on, May, lets have some tea. He'll be back. *(He sighs.)* I don't know what you'd do without me to sort out all your problems.

SCENE 3

*(**Drew** is sitting on a wall looking down onto the football pitch that lies at the back of the estate. Between taking drinks from a can of Coke, he speaks his thoughts out loud.)*

Drew   I don't care! I don't care what Eddie says, I'm glad I gave Bobby beats. He shouldn't have said those things, just 'cos we wouldn't join his all black gang. That would have meant that next we couldn't play with Mikey . . . Why did I bother standing up for him though? It only got me into trouble with Eddie. I bet if my real dad still lived with us I would've got away with ripping Bobby's jacket . . . They all make me sick. I don't know why I don't just go and join Bobby's gang, I'm just about the right colour, but he wouldn't let me now, not even if I got his jacket mended. I hate this place!

(He chucks the Coke can at the wire fence around the pitch and it clatters to the ground.)

SCENE 4

(*Clive* and *Gill King's* house in the suburbs of the city. It is 7.30 in the morning. *Gill* comes into the kitchen looking for her daughter, *Holly*.)

Gill   Holly, are you in the garden?

(*Holly* walks in through the back door.)

Holly   I was! What's wrong with the daffodils this year? They're all small and puny looking.

Gill   Holly, please wipe your feet before coming in from the garden. You've dirtied my clean kitchen floor.

Holly   Sorry.

(She sits at the table. *Gill* starts to prepare breakfast.)

Holly   I think I'll start planting some summer bulbs now. It's about time.

Gill   That's a good idea. We can do it on Saturday afternoon. What do you want for breakfast?

Holly   Can I ask Sarah and Nicky around after school?

Gill   I thought you were going riding with them today?

Holly   Yeah, but they can come over after. I'm always going to their house after riding.

Gill   Oh no no no, I've got Pat coming around this afternoon. I want you at riding, so I can have a quiet house. I don't want loads of girls rampaging through the place.

Holly   But . . .

Gill   No!

(There's a silence.)

Holly   What's Pat coming round for anyway?

Gill   Well, I might as well tell you now, though I was going to save it as a surprise for you and Dad at dinner tonight. Pat and I want to start a little business. She'll do the machine work; altering people's clothes and curtains and coats, and I'll do the advertising, getting customers, keeping the books, and so on. She's going to take a look at the spare room and see if it's big enough for her to work in. I think it will be just right.

(The front door slams and **Clive** *comes through into the kitchen, with a bundle of letters in his hand.)*

Clive Morning, morning everyone!

Gill Morning, love. Sit down and I'll get you your coffee. Did you open up the shop OK?

Clive Yes. No problems. And how are you this morning, young lady?

Holly All right.

(**Clive** *sits at the table. He begins to open the letters.)*

Clive Good. Gill, you know that paper boy, Darren? Wasn't it you who told me to take him on?

Gill Yes. I know his mother. She's a very nice woman.

Clive Well, this is the second day in a row he hasn't turned up. I rang his house and his sister had to go and get him out of bed.

Holly He's in my class. He's always late for school.

Clive You see, Gill.

(He reads the letter.)

Gill I thought he would be all right because his mother seems decent. In fact, she was the one who introduced me to Pat at the sewing circle.

Clive Mm.

(**Gill** *comes to the table with coffee and toast.)*

Gill Talking of Pat . . . I'm seeing her this afternoon. I'm going to pick her up in the car.

(**Clive** *mutters under his breath.)*

Gill You're not using the car this afternoon are you? I thought I'd bring her over here, since this is where she'll probably be working.

*(**Clive** hasn't heard her. He's too absorbed in his letter.)*

Clive   I thought something like this would happen one day.

Gill   How could you? I only had the idea a few days ago, and I haven't told anyone, except for Holly and that was just before you came in. Don't you think it's an exciting idea? The business side could be a real doddle. We could merge it with the shop.

*(**Clive** is still reading.)*

Gill   Don't worry! I'd do all our figures. You wouldn't have to do a thing. The only obstacle now is to find a workshop for Pat. I . . . I was thinking of converting the spare room.

*(**Clive** puts down the letter.)*

Clive   Drew must be in a bad way to write me a letter like that. I think maybe we should have him here for a little while. He can sleep in the spare room.

*(**Gill's** smile vanishes, but **Holly** looks from her mother to her father with a huge grin.)*

SCENE 5

*(**Holly** paces around the large lawn at the back of the house, bypassing the swing, the fish pond and the cedar tree. She speaks her thoughts.)*

Holly   So he's coming to stay! Maybe!! I wish it was Tina or Dawn, but Drew is better than no one. I wonder what he's like now. It's been ages since I last saw him. It's going to be great. When mum says my friends can't come round, it won't matter because there'll always be someone to play with in the garden. I'll have Drew here. My brother!

(She hears her parents talking inside the house and crosses the garden to listen at the open window.)

Gill   It's not that I don't want the boy here, Clive. I just feel we ought to think about the situation before we make any rash promises.

Clive   I have thought about it. Have you read his letter?

Gill   No.

Clive Then listen! *(Reading.)* 'Every time Mikey does something bad he gets away with it and when I'm meant to have done something bad, I don't. It's because we aren't a proper family with a real dad. There's only Eddie, and mum NEVER STANDS UP FOR ME IN FRONT OF HIM. No one ever thinks about me! Not even Mikey, when he clutters up half my room with all the stuff Eddie buys for him. It ain't fair . . .' *(He stops reading.)* Isn't it obvious that the boy is unhappy?

Gill The whole thing might have blown over by now. You know what children are like.

Clive I'll 'phone him today and see how he is. I think he should come and stay.

Gill Have you thought about Holly? This is her home as well. How is she going to feel about one of your other children living here?

*(**Clive** comes to the window. He knows **Holly** is standing there.)*

Clive Ask her!

Gill Holly! Have you been listening?

Holly Yes!

Gill Oh, dear . . . Well, let's hear what you think? Do you want Drew to stay?

Holly Great!

Gill Oh!

Clive There you are. Look Gill, I know you're thinking of this business idea of yours, and that you need that room, so what I suggest is that we have Drew here during the holidays and see how it goes. If it works out and he wants to stay, then we'll have to look for somewhere else for you and Pat. If it doesn't work, then you can have the spare room. No problem! OK?

Gill Mm.

Clive It's the least I can do. I am his father. That man Eddie is no good, or so Drew says. And May would be the kind of woman to get herself into a bad situation like that and stay in it, because she's too lazy to get out. She's not like you Gill, all get up and go. Maybe you're the kind of example that Drew needs at a time like this.

Gill   Yes, Clive. You may be right.

SCENE 5

*(A few days later. **Gill** is driving **Drew** home from the railway station.)*

Gill   So what did May say when you told her that you wanted to come and live with your dad?

Drew   She tried saying that I couldn't swap families and that dad might not want me. She said that I wasn't being loyal to her after all she had done for me. Then she cried.

Gill   She has done a lot for you. Why did you want to leave?

Drew   That lot just get me sick.

Gill   Why? There must be a reason.

Drew   You wouldn't understand.

Gill   Try me.

Drew   Well, some black kids on our estate were going around all the half-black kids saying, 'Are you black, or are you white?' I said I was neither. They started calling me and my sisters names, so I beat one of them up, and Eddie told me off and punished me. He's always doing that. He's white, and he's always letting Mikey get away with everything . . . and Mikey's white, and my mum never stands up for me . . . and she's white, so I reckoned white let me down.

Gill   But Drew, their colour's probably got nothing to do with the way they treat you.

Drew   I knew you wouldn't understand. It *has* got something to do with it. I thought I'd best be black, and come and live with Dad, 'cos he's black, and he'll treat me the same way Eddie treats Mikey.

Gill   So that's what you think, is it?

Drew Yeah, it is.

Gill Well, we'll just have to wait and see won't we. Oh look, there's Holly's school. You'll have to go there if you carry on living with us after the holidays.

Drew No way, man, I'm getting the train back to my own school. It's only an hour away.

Gill We don't know if your school is going to allow that, when you can transfer to this one quite easily . . . Over there is the church hall where Holly does tap and ballet. Have you got any hobbies, Drew?

Drew Ride my bike.

Gill That's not exactly a hobby.

Drew Better than tap dancing.

Gill It's an interest and I think it's important that all children have an interest. It's a golden rule in our house. We could get you gardening with Holly, or even bird watching. There's lots of places where you can do that around here.

Drew Yeah I bet, but I ain't going to.

Gill You must do what we say, or you can't be part of our family.

Drew Look, there's my dad's shop!

Gill *Our* shop.

Drew I wanna go and see him.

Gill Not at the moment. It's not very convenient. He's busy this afternoon checking the stock and that always makes him bad tempered. You don't want to see him in that kind of mood.

(She slows down the car and stops.)

Gill But there again, maybe you **should** see the other sides of your dad.

*(**Drew** is already out of the car and running into the shop.)*

SCENE 6

*(In the King's shop. **Clive** and **Rita**, his shop assistant, are checking boxes and trying to serve at the same time. **Clive** is reading from a*

stock list. *The local* **vicar** *is peering into a fridge at the back of the shop.*)

Clive   There should be two hundred Mars Bars.

Rita   Right.

Vicar   How much is this block of vanilla ice cream, Rita?

Rita   I'm not sure.

Clive   Have a look at the list on the freezer, Vicar.

Vicar   Will do!

Clive   Rita, is there a box of two hundred Kit Kat?

Rita   Sure is.

Vicar   And have you got *Dogs' World* in yet, Clive?

Clive   Yes, on the third shelf.

(**Clive** *is still checking his list.*)

Clive   And two hundred Benson and Hedges?

Rita   Er, can't see them here.

(**Drew** *comes into the shop.*)

Drew   Hi Dad!

Clive   Drew! Why ain't you with Gill? She didn't get you from the station?

Drew   Yeah, she did.

Vicar   I can't see any copies up here, Clive.

Clive   Try the shelf below.

Drew   I thought *you* were going to come?

Clive   Come where?

Rita   Mr King, I've checked. There's no Benson and Hedges.

Clive   Not again. This happens nearly every week.

Drew   I thought you were going to come to the station, Dad.

Clive Look Drew, I would've if I could. This shop opens at seven and closes at nine and someone's got to run the business, or we don't get no money to live.

Rita Shall I phone the warehouse?

Clive Yeah, do that.

Vicar Is this your son, Clive?

Clive Yes. He's come to stay for a while.

Vicar We'll have to get him to come and join my Scout pack.

Drew Rather ride my bike.

Vicar Bit dangerous?

Drew Yeah, it is at the moment 'cos my tyres are bust.

Rita The warehouse is engaged.

Clive Keep on trying.

Rita All right.

Drew I thought you might buy me some, Dad.

Clive Buy you what?

Drew Tyres.

Clive You must be joking man! You've only been here five minutes and you're already asking for money. Jesus Christ! Oh sorry, Vicar.

Drew Sorry, Dad.

Vicar Eureka! I've found it! *Dogs' World.* So . . . I'll take that, and the ice cream, and a packet of my peppermints. And have you any idea when we can expect the morning papers to be delivered again?

Clive Yes, Vicar, I have! *(To **Drew**).* Drew, if you want some new tyres for your bike, you'll have to work for the money. As from tomorrow, you're my new paper boy.

SCENE 7

*(A week later in the Kings' garden. **Holly** has a bag of bulbs, which she is showing **Drew**.)*

Holly These are begonias and they have to be planted with that pointed bit, there, sticking out of the soil. Put them in a row along the front of this bed about five inches apart, and make sure the soil's packed tightly around them. When they come up, they'll be really pretty – all pink, yellow and white. I want to put some night-scented stock in between them as well. D'you know what that is?

Drew OXO?

(**Holly** *laughs and turns away to another flower-bed. She doesn't see* **Drew** *get onto the swing.*)

Holly No, silly! It's this tiny flower that grows in a sort of bush, and in the evening, it gives out this lovely smell. You'll really like it.

(*She turns to face him.*)

Holly Drew, why aren't you helping me?

Drew It's boring.

Holly No, it's not . . . I know, when we've done this, we could take some of dad's planks, and build a den behind his shed where no one can see.

Drew Let's do it now.

Holly But what about the plants? We can't just leave them half-finished. I thought you wanted to do some gardening. That's what Mum said.

Drew You thought wrong then, didn't you? Gill made me come out here to have a hobby. She wouldn't let me ride my bike after we had our tea. She said I had to let it digest. The food was horrible. It won't digest. It tasted like cardboard. Your mum don't put no spices in her food like my mum does.

Holly It tasted all right to me. Anyway, why d'you want to ride your bike again? You've been here nearly a week and all you ever want to do is ride your bike.

Drew So? You're always in the garden.

Holly I've hardly seen you since you came.

Drew   I've hardly seen my dad since I came.

Holly   No one ever sees Dad 'cos he's always at the shop. But what about me? I'm here.

Drew   Yeah, but where's all the other kids? There's no one around in this place. Listen . . . it's so quiet.

Holly   Mum doesn't like it when I bring friends around. She says we make the place untidy. So I see them when I go riding.

Drew   Riding what?

Holly   My horse.

Drew   You got a horse?

Holly   Yeah, Mum and Dad bought it for me.

Drew   Did they? You lucky thing! . . . You ain't got no friends though.

Holly   Yes I have, Nicky and Sarah.

Drew   Oh brilliant, you've got two friends. On the estate where I live, there's loads of kids that's my friends; big ones, little ones, boys, girls, black, white, mixed, Indian, Chinese . . . loads of them. I bet your two friends are white, aren't they?

Holly   Yeah.

Drew   Got any black kids in your school?

Holly   I've seen an Indian boy.

Drew   Only one! Na, man, there's no way Gill's getting me to go your school.

Holly   But why?

Drew   Don't you feel funny?

Holly   Only when I first went there. They kept asking me if I was adopted.

Drew   That's 'cos you're the only black person in your class.

Holly   I'm not black.

Drew   Yes you are.

Holly   I'm not the same colour as Dad.

Drew   You're not the same colour as Gill either.

Holly   I nearly am.

Drew   So you choose to be white. Bobby Moss would call you dirty white.

Holly   Who's Bobby Moss?

Drew   This black kid on our estate who goes round making kids like us choose if they're black or white.

Holly   What did you choose?

Drew   Black of course, like Dad.

Holly   But you don't even know Dad properly.

Drew   All I know is that he must be better than my mum.

Holly   It's the other way around with me.

(*Gill calls from an upstairs window.*)

Gill   Holly love, do you want to come up and have a look at some dresses Pat has just brought round?

Holly   Yeah.

(*She runs indoors.*)

Drew   Girls always side with their mums!

SCENE 8

(*A couple of days later at the Kings' house.* **Clive** *comes through the front door, slamming it behind him. He stands at the foot of the stairs and shouts.*)

Clive   Drew! Drew!

(**Holly** *comes downstairs.*)

Clive   Where is Drew?

(**Drew** *comes from the kitchen, followed by* **Gill.**)

Drew   What is it Dad?

Gill   Is everything all right at the shop?

Clive   Yes.

Gill   Good. And before you say anything else, did you know that the fence behind the shed has nearly fallen down? You must have put your planks up against it.

Drew   That was Holly.

Holly   We were going to build a den, but then you called me in to see those dresses. When I came out, Drew had gone off on his bike, so I built it . . .

(*Clive has been waiting for them to finish. Now he loses his patience.*)

Clive   Forget the fence! It's nothing! We can can easily pay for that. There's more serious things we've got to discuss . . . like Drew smashing Mrs Roberts' front window.

Gill   What?!

Clive   I couldn't believe it when she rang the shop and told me. He did it this morning when he was delivering her paper, didn't you, Drew?

Drew   But she called me a darkie! She said, 'Put the newspaper right through the letter box, darkie'.

Clive   I don't care what she called you. These are our neighbours and our customers, and you don't go around smashing their windows.

Drew   But Dad, say she called you it? You can understand can't you? She's racist.

Clive   You're gonna meet a hell of a lot of people like Mrs Roberts in the world. You can't box them all down. Sticks and stones, remember! Now, I've told her that you're gonna put some of your wages towards mending her window.

Drew   I thought you would've agreed with me, but you're punishing me, just like Eddie did. I thought 'cos you were black like me that you'd stand up for me, but you've just let me down, like mum.

Clive   Colour's got nothing to do with it, Drew.

Drew It ain't fair. You stick up for Holly. You bought her a
horse. You wouldn't even buy me any tyres . . . and she don't
even think she's black like you. You lot get me sick as well!

(*Drew runs into the garden.* **Holly** *follows.*)

Gill Holly, come back! . . . Oh, I can't understand the boy. I told
you this situation wouldn't work out, Clive.

(**Holly** *screams from the garden.*)

Holly Drew stop it! Stop it!

Gill What now . . . what's he up to?

(**Holly** *runs back into the house.*)

Holly Mum! Dad! Stop him! He's kicking up all the flowers that I
planted. Stop him!

(*They run into the garden.*)

SCENE 9

(*At the Jacks' house.* **May** *and* **Eddie** *are watching television in the
kitchen.*)

May That was a new jumper that Mikey came home in after he'd
been to stay with his mum.

Eddie She only bought that for him because I sent him down there
in some new trainers. She thinks she can outdo me by buying
the boy's affection, but it won't work. I earn far more than she
does, and Mikey knows what side his bread is buttered on.

May Eddie, it's no good carrying on this way with Mikey. He's
just going to be playing you off, one against the other. And all
the time you're playing games with her, *this* family . . . your
new family . . . is suffering. Look! Just look at us. We're
already split up, with Drew gone off to his dad's, just
because . . .

(*There is a light tap on the door.* **Eddie** *gets up to answer it.*)

Eddie Saved by the knock!!

May   You might joke about it, Eddie, but I think these things have to be said.

*(**Eddie** opens the door. **Drew** is standing outside, carrying a suitcase.)*

Eddie   Gordon Bennet! Look who it is May! The Wanderer has returned.

*(**May** gets up to hug **Drew** as he comes in.)*

May   Drew! What's going on!? What's happened? Why didn't you tell us you were coming back?

Drew   I thought you might say you never wanted me.

May   Don't be daft. I'm really happy you've come home. But what happened?

Eddie   Have a fight, did you?

Drew   No.

Eddie   Did Gill get fed up living with other people's kids?

May   That's enough, Eddie. I think I've had just about enough of putting up with your unfair judgement in this house, and with all the trouble it causes.

Eddie   If you think I've been unfair, why haven't you said anything?

May   I only put up with it to save arguments between us, because I didn't want this marriage to split up like my last one did. Now I don't care; it's about time I said something.

Eddie   Come on then, let's hear it. What have I done?

May   You've got to start treating these kids all the same, or we can't be a proper family. Drew and Tina and Dawn aren't always bad and they don't always deserve all the punishment. And Mikey isn't always good and shouldn't get all the favours. Things aren't just black and white like that.

Drew   Thanks Mum. That's a start . . .

May   Things take a long time to sort themselves out, especially the important things. Remember that, Drew.

*(There is a frantic banging at the front door and the other children rush in. With them is their dog, Jay Jay. He jumps up at **Drew** and licks his face.)*

Mikey Drew!

Dawn Great! You're back!

Tina Bobby Moss won't leave us alone!

Mikey And he's saying I can't play with them. Cor! I'm glad you're back!

*(**Drew** runs to the door and calls out over the balcony.)*

Drew Bobby Moss, leave us alone! This family ain't calling themselves one colour or another! We're just calling ourselves the Jacks! Right!

(He slams the door shut. The others cheer.)

Talking Points

(For discussion in small groups, write each 'Talking Point' on a separate piece of card.)

A lot of things could be about to change for the Jacks family. Drew has returned. May is firmly on his side. Eddie is being challenged about the way he treats the family. Bobby Moss has been put in his place.

So . . . what do you think will happen now?

Will Drew and his mother draw ever closer?

Will Eddie be able to treat Drew and Mikey the same?

Will Drew continue to see his real father?

Will Bobby Moss finally stop bullying Drew and his sisters?

Investigations

1. If Drew was asked to write an essay called 'The person I most respect', whom would he choose? At different times in the play he might choose different people; for example, his mother, Holly, and even Bobby Moss.

Choose a time in Drew's story and write this essay for him.

Who'll win the title of 'most respected person'?

Give as many reasons as you can for respecting this person. Write as Drew, not as yourself.

2. As the play ends, it seems that life is going to be different from now on in the Jacks' household. Choose one member of the family and try to see things from their point of view. Make up an entry for a diary or a short letter to a friend, written by your character on the evening of Drew's return. What are your hopes for the future? Why might things be different now? You may also want to write about any fears that you have. Do you think everyone will stick to their promises?

3. You may have heard the expression: 'It's not what you say, it's the way that you say it'. The same words can sometimes carry an entirely different message if you say them in a different tone of voice. Look at the following piece of dialogue. It's not in the script, but if it was, it might appear where Drew finally decides that he's had enough of the Kings' household and that he's going back to his mum and his sisters. It would follow on from the scene (page 90) where Drew storms off into the garden and tears up Holly's bulbs.

> **Clive** So, that's it then . . . home to May. That's your choice, is it Drew?
>
> **Gill** I'm not pushing you out. Stay if you want. Pat and I will find somewhere else to work.
>
> **Holly** There's a lot of bulbs to be replanted.
>
> **Drew** I'm going home!

In groups of four, work out a scene that ends with the dialogue written above. Decide whether the characters speak those lines in a sad way, or in anger, or in a different tone altogether. Your choice will obviously be decided by what happens in the early part of your scene and you'll have to create the right sort of atmosphere to lead up to the closing lines. Look back through the script (particularly pages 88–90) to refresh your memory about the events leading up to this missing dialogue. When you've had a chance to rehearse, show your version to the rest of the class. What differences are there between each group's version of the scene?

4. At first, Drew is pleased to be staying with his dad. His dad will stick up for him – or so Drew thinks.

In pairs or threes, act out the 'phone call that Drew makes to one or both of his sisters a few days after he's arrived at his dad's house. How will Drew be feeling? How will he want his sisters to react?

5. The family structure in *Jacks and Kings* is a very complex one. (Try to explain it to a partner and see how clearly you can do it!) It may be easier to see the whole network of relationships in a diagram. Make a

Family Tree for the Jacks and Kings, showing who is now married to whom, and how the children of the various marriages are related to each other.

6. There's a great deal of conflict in *Jacks and Kings*, particularly when family and racial loyalties are put to the test. The story might make good material for a comic strip in a teenage magazine. As the artist of that comic strip, choose one of the more dramatic moments from the play and illustrate it in comic strip form. Be economical! Try to get your message across in just a few pictures. Give each picture appropriate captions or speech 'bubbles'.

CATCH-MAN

Janys Chambers

THE CHARACTERS

WOMEN

The women who make things:

Grey, one of the oldest Women in the Nunkertown. Very experienced, unusually open-minded, wise and calm

Wilder, a young Woman. Passionate and artistic

The women who guard the area from attack:

Maze, not physically strong, but supported by the other Women. Gentle

Moon, brisk and efficient

The women who teach the girls:

Flight, a quiet but firm personality

Stone, confident in her opinions, likes to talk

BOY

Richard, likeable, but a bit inclined to strut and swagger

GIRLS

Flinty, one of the oldest Girls. The natural leader of the whole group, intelligent and strong

Riji, an older Girl. Very clever this one. Very sharp, very watchful

Willow, does everything by the rules

Black, a little younger than Flinty, Riji and Willow. Strong, brave, daring, a bit too quick to make up her mind sometimes; given to recklessness, a bit wild

Cat, admires Black, but would be surprised to learn that Black admires her. Quiet, warm, very compassionate, but uses her head too

Arrow, a peace-maker. The go-between for Cat and Black

Fox, the youngest Girl and the pet of the group. Very open and direct

Bone, Fox's particular friend. Has a good sense of humour

About this play

The play is set in the future after a nuclear war, in a non-contaminated area, a Nunkertown, which is probably somewhere in Australia – though this is not important. The inhabitants of this particular Nunkertown are all female. They are descendants of both natives and refugees of the nuclear holocaust. Language has survived, but in an altered form. The language they use is called Nunkertese.

You may find it difficult to read and understand, at first, but stick with it!! You'll find that part of the fun of acting out the script comes from trying to decipher this strange language. If you get really stuck, you'll find help in the vocabulary list on pages 125–127, but try to get through the play without consulting it. Later, you can check whether your understanding of the words matches those that are given in the list.

SCENE 1

(Morning. A craggy hillside rising out of some carefully cultivated land (the 'plant') where some scrubby fruit bushes and a few vegetables are struggling to grow. There is a cave opening in the hillside. Eight girls run on. They have come to play the game 'catch-men', like our 'hide and seek', in which the hiders are called 'men', the seekers are called 'catchers', and the safe den is called 'edge'. They are looking for a place to be the dungeon or 'home' for the 'men' who are caught. They see the cave.)

Flinty   Look. Look! This place do!

Cat   Cave-Place! Yes!

Arrow   Yes!

Fox   This be Home.

(They peer inside the cave.)

Fox   How long this Cave-Place go?

(They cannot see to the back of the cave.)

Flinty   Longer than my eyes, Fox.

Bone   Long as rope.

Cat   We need carry Fire inside, see how long.

Fox   Make Fire now!

Willow   May be Animal-Place.

Riji   May have broken roof. May have broken floor. May be Old-Time Mine. *(She shivers.)* Man-Place.

Black   Seeing is knowing. Us go inside.

(She starts to make fire.)

Flinty   No. Fire take Long-Time. See inside Cave-Place After-Day. Yes! Come with Fire-Pot from Village After-Day! Now, play Catch-Men!

Riji   Yes! Play Catch-Men now!

*(**Fox** points to the cave.)*

Fox   This be Home!

Bone *(chanting gleefully)*   Men have brought us trouble and woe. Down into this Home they go!

*(**Riji** points to a tree twenty metres away.)*

Riji   That tree! That tree be Edge!

Arrow   Who be Catchers, who be Men?

Black *(quickly)*   Me be Man, me be Man!

Riji *(resentfully)*   Before-Day, in Plague-Game, you be Plague. This-day, in Catch-Men, you be Man.

Bone   Next-Day, in Next-Game, you be left in Village!

(They laugh.)

Cat *(helpfully)*   Me be Man *or* Catcher. Me be Catcher.

Arrow   And me.

Flinty   No. Fair choosing. Fox, get pebble.

*(**Fox** finds a pebble with two different sides and shows it to everyone. Then she tosses it into the air. It falls some way off.)*

Flinty   Side-Up be Men, Side-Down be Catchers. Dapple or Grey?

Black   Dapple.

Fox   Grey.

Arrow   Dapple.

Riji   Dapple.

Willow   Dapple.

Cat   Dapple.

Bone   Grey.

Flinty   Grey.

   (They run and look to see how the pebble has landed.)

Fox   Grey.

Willow   Greys be Men, Dapples be Catchers.

Black   More Catchers than Men. Good.

Cat   Like in Real-Time.

Riji   So, Catchers count Twenty-War.

Fox   Yes. One-War, Two-War . . .

Black   You Men Go-Hide but . . .

Willow *(interrupting)*   Keeping on paths.

Black   Go no longer than Plant.

Willow   And keeping on paths. Careful of Food growing!

Bone   Oh, Willow, you on Teaching?

Arrow   Twenty-War we Come-Look.

Cat   We catch you . . .

Black   We put you in Home.

Arrow   But you touch that tree, you reach Edge . . .

Riji   We Men go free!

Fox   Yes!

Bone   Over Edge escape our foe,
      Only-Place that Men now know.

Flinty Begin.

(The 'catchers' close their eyes and begin counting.)

Riji
Black
Cat } One-War, Two-War, Three-War, Four-War . . .
Arrow
Willow

(The 'men' start running.)

Fox Quick!

Bone Come on Fox!

Riji
Black
Cat } Five-War, Six-War, Seven-War, Eight-War . . .
Arrow
Willow

Fox Where's Flinty?

Flinty *(calling)* Over here!

Bone Over there.

Riji
Black
Cat } Nine-War, Ten-War, Eleven-War . . .
Arrow
Willow

Bone Me go this way.

Riji
Black
Cat } Twelve-War, Thirteen-War, Fourteen-War, Fifteen-
War . . .
Arrow
Willow

Flinty *(calling)* Run Fox!

Riji
Black
Cat } Sixteen-War, Seventeen-War, Eighteen-War . . .
Arrow
Willow

Fox   Not ready, not ready!

Riji
Black
Cat } Nineteen-War . . .
Arrow
Willow

Bone   SSh!

Riji
Black
Cat } Twenty-War . . .
Arrow
Willow

Fox   Not –

Riji
Black
Cat } Ready!
Arrow
Willow

(**Fox** *bolts for edge first.*)

Riji   There go Fox. Quick, quick!

Black   Get her, get her!

(*They chase and catch her.*)

Arrow
Cat } Got you! Into Home with you!
Willow

(**Black** *sits on* **Fox** *who giggles, while* **Cat** *and* **Arrow** *bind her wrists and ankles. They lift her into the air.*)

100   **Black**   Watch for Bone and Flinty!

*(They lift **Fox** and toss her laughing three times into the air, before lowering her into the mouth of the cave.)*

Cat ⎤ *(chanting)* Men have brought us trouble and woe.
Arrow ⎦ Down into this Home they go!

*(**Bone** is trying to creep up to 'edge'.)*

Arrow　Get Bone, Riji!

Black　Run, Riji!

*(**Riji** tags **Bone**, and she and **Black** carry her over and repeat the ritual of placing her in the cave.)*

Riji ⎤ Men have brought us trouble and woe.
Black ⎦ Down into this Home they go!

Fox *(giggling)*　Bone, Bone, we be in Home forever!

Willow　Catch Flinty now.

Black　We Go-Look.

Riji　No. Scatter like seed and she come. Flinty be sharp as teeth.

Cat　Best on Guarding.

Arrow　And watching.

Black　Just go short way then.

*(She goes one way, **Willow** another. **Riji**, **Cat** and **Arrow** stay on guard by the cave. **Bone** calls from the cave.)*

Bone　Dark in here!

Fox　When you feed us?

Cat *(calling back)*　After-Day!

Riji *(calling back)*　After-Day in Cold-Time!

Arrow　There she go!

*(**Flinty** dashes between **Black** and **Willow**. Those by the cave are not quick enough to stop her.)*

Flinty　Edge! Edge!

Riji　See. Sharp as teeth.

Arrow   Still. Have two in Home . . .

Black   Yes. Two Men. *(Teasing.)* Two Bad Men.

*(She goes into the cave and tickles **Fox** and **Bone**.)*

Fox   Help! Leave-Alone!

Bone   Leave-Alone! Leave-Alone! Not Breeding-Time!

*(**Arrow, Cat, Riji** and **Willow** join the others in the cave. They all sit. The two 'men' are untied.)*

Flinty   Knock? Outsider enter?

Cat   Peace.

*(**Flinty** joins them.)*

Flinty   Near High-Sun.

Cat   Cool in this Cave-Place.

Fox   Cave-Place Mine in Old-Time?

Riji   Maybe.

Fox *(shivering)*   Man-Place . . .

Riji   Men digging for gold.

Fox   Gold. Cold gold .˙. .

Willow   For ornaments. And Food-Bowls.

Fox *(dreamily)*   Cold-Gold from Cool-Cave. There be Ghosts here?

Riji   Maybe. Yes. Ghosts.

Black   Old-Time Ghosts. Man-Ghosts.

Arrow   With diggers in hand.

Black   For killing with.

Cat   Black! Men kill, not Ghosts, Fox.

Willow   Food-Time soon.

Flinty   Yes. Who for Village?

Riji   Me.

Fox Me.

Bone Race you, Fox.

Flinty Black?

Black Soon.

Flinty *(warning)* Near High-Sun.

Black Soon!

Cat Me wait with Black.

Arrow And me.

Flinty See after.

*(Five of them go. **Arrow, Cat** and **Black** remain.)*

Arrow Cool this Cave-Place.

Cat Look at Plant, land, stretching Long-Away.

Arrow Village too Long-Away for my eyes.

Cat And me.

Black Ghost eyes maybe seeing it. *(She laughs.)*

Cat Bad Black, making Bad dreams for Fox.

Arrow *(scornfully)* Ghosts killing! Bad Black.

*(**Black** laughs again. There is a sudden noise at the back of the cave.)*

Cat What . . . ?

Black Ssh!

Arrow What . . . ?

Black Ssh!

(They freeze. There is silence. Then they speak in whispers.)

Arrow You hear that?

Cat Yes.

(They listen. More silence.)

Black Go-Look.

Cat   With no Fire?

Black   Come.

(They creep forward into the dark back of the cave.)

Cat   It be dark.

Arrow   Go back.

Black   No!

(Suddenly she grabs hold of cat.)

Black   Look!

(There is a shape ahead of them in the darkness. They freeze again.)

Cat   Animal?

Arrow   Leave-Alone.

Black   No.

Arrow   Leave-Alone!

Black   No!

*(**Black** steps forward. **Cat** steps with her. The shape suddenly lunges at them and they run to the mouth of the cave, uncertain for a moment whether to keep on running or to turn back and face it. They turn back. The shape has stopped in the dim light near the cave-mouth.)*

Cat   It be Girl!

Richard   No. Not Girl. Boy.

Arrow   Boy!

Richard   Right! And Boy have knife, right?

(He points the knife at them. For the first time they are really frightened.)

Cat   Boy drop knife.

Richard   No.

Cat   Boy, you have one knife. Kill one Girl, other two jump.

(He stares at them.)

Arrow   Drop knife.

Richard   No.

Black   No killing here.

Richard   No!

(*Cat raises her arms slowly in a wide gesture.*)

Cat   Peace.

(*There is a pause. The boy drops the knife and starts to cry.* **Arrow** *snatches up the knife.*)

Black   Man-Child! Killer! Why we stopped you Long-Time, put you in Home, always killing. Killer!

Richard   I not killer!

Black   Then why this knife, killer?

Richard   I not killer, right?

Arrow   Where you from, Boy?

(*Before he can answer,* **Black** *speaks . . .*)

Black   From over Edge. Call Guarders.

(*She reaches for a whistle made from bamboo.*)

Richard   No!

Cat   Wait. Where you from, Boy?

Richard   Outside. I make tunnel under wall, tunnel in.

Arrow   See no Guarders?

Richard   No. Before, I always see them by wall. I come out tunnel, I see no Guarders, right, I run and run and run till here.

Arrow   Tunnelling under Edge!

Black   Show us! Show us tunnel!

Richard   Tunnel lost. Tunnel lost, Richard lost. You killing Richard now? Right?

(*He starts to cry.*)

Cat (*gently*)   No killing here. Richard. Richard your name?

(The boy nods.)

Arrow   Richard.

Cat   Boy-Name. My name Cat. This Arrow, this Black.

Arrow   Take her Village.

Cat   'Him'. Boys 'him', not 'her'.

Arrow   Him. Come on.

*(**Arrow** and **Black** take hold of him.)*

Richard   No!

(He starts to struggle.)

Richard   No!!

(They are stronger than he is. He subsides in their grip.)

Richard   What your Village do?

Black   Kill you!

Cat   No!

Arrow   No. We do not kill, only if being killed.

Richard   They let I go home?

Arrow   Home?

Black   This Home here, maybe. Shut you away with all Men. No going back.

Arrow   No! Go-Back, you bring more Outsiders.

Richard   No. You keep I, more come, right? My family. My family Come-Look.

Cat   Family?

(They are puzzled.)

Richard   Family. Who live with I, you know. My father, my mother, right?

Cat   His Birth-Mother.

Arrow   You live with her?

Richard   Yes. Look, take this book.

(He takes a picture-book out of a small knapsack.)

Richard   Take it. Take my bag. Anything.

(The girls stare at the book.)

Cat   You carry this book?

(She takes it.)

Richard   Yes, it be mine, right?

Cat *(she does not understand the word 'mine')*   'Mine'?

Richard   Yes, mine, you know. My Book. You have no Old-Time Books?

Cat   Yes, but in Teaching-Place, for all. Women Come-Look. Not having All-Time. Not carrying.

Richard   Well, have it. For All-Time. But let I go home.

Black   What your Home?

Richard   Like all homes. No. Not like yours, Shut-Away Place. Please. Please. Let I go, right?

Arrow   Law say no.

Black   Take her Village.

Arrow   Him!

Cat   No. Him frightened.

Black   Law say.

Cat   First Law, Caring.

(There is a sound beyond the cave.)

Flinty *(calling)*   Black! Arrow!

Cat   They coming back. Hide him!

Black   No.

Cat   While we think. Back of cave.

Black   No. Men killers.

Arrow We have his knife.

Flinty *(calling)* Cat! Black!

Cat Black, we talk him more. Like secret. Like in story. For Short-Time!

*(From outside the cave come the voices of **Fox** and **Bone**.)*

Fox They be eat up. Ghost-Food.

Bone Just Bone left.

(They laugh.)

Cat *(pleading)* Black?

Black *(turning to Arrow)* Arrow?

Arrow Yes.

Black Short-Time then.

*(She turns to **Richard**.)*

Black Boy, you Want-Live?

(He nods.)

Black You hide. You come out, we all take you Village.

*(**Richard** runs to the back of the cave. **Riji** and **Flinty** come in.)*

Flinty You lost ears, Black?

*(**Black** doesn't answer.)*

Riji Lost tongue, too, Flinty.

*(Still the three do not speak. **Riji** looks at them all, puzzled. They are standing rooted to the spot in the mouth of the cave.)*

Cat We . . . it be Food-Time?

Riji Nearer than Before-Time.

Fox We come get you, go Village, play Cross-World on way.

Arrow Yes, Cross-World.

Black Yes. Go then.

(She raises her voice.)

Black   Leave Ghosts stay in Cave-Place.

Riji   You see Ghosts, Black?

Cat *(hurriedly)*   We talking Ghosts, Riji. Man-Ghosts.

*(**Riji** throws her a sharp look, then looks back into the cave. She can see nothing. They all step out into the sun. **Willow** and **Arrow** are there. It is very hot now.)*

Willow   So. Cross-World. This way round . . .

(She gestures round the group.)

Willow   One word each. Who get 'OUT' lose arm. Say where words start next.

Fox   Who get next 'OUT' lose other arm.

Willow   Then leg . . .

Fox   Hopping!

Willow   Then other leg . . .

Fox   Crawling!

Willow   Then out game.

Bone   Worm-Person, crawling back Village!

Flinty   Who get back with most body win. Ready?

Arrow   Ready.

Flinty   Begin.

All *(chanting)*   Cross-World-All-Body
  Cross-Sea-All-Body
  Cross-Desert-All-Body
  Noddy-Noddy-No-Body
  No-Body-Spells-Out.

(The chant fades into the distance.)

All   Cross-World-All-Body
  Cross-Sea-All-Body
  Cross-Desert-All-Body
  Noddy-Noddy-No-Body
  No-Body-Spells-Out.

Richard   All alone. All alone. (*He shivers.*) All alone.

(*A long silence. Then he hears a noise. He retreats terrified to the back of the cave. Footsteps approach the cave. **Richard** wants to scream, but stuffs his hand into his mouth.*)

Cat   Richard. Richard! Me, Cat.

(*Slowly he relaxes, inches forward. They see each other.*)

Cat   Me come back. Say, stone in foot.

Richard   I think Ghosts. Ghosts with diggers Come-Kill I. For gold.

(*He starts to cry.*)

Richard   In here, Ghosts. Out there, Guarders, place where you kill I, place where you shut I away. That Black . . .

Cat   She help you.

Richard   Help shut I away, right?

Cat   Maybe. After-Sun, we have Meet.

Richard   I hungry.

Cat   Bring some food. (*She touches him.*) And covering.

Richard   You help I?

Cat   Yes.

Richard   Help I go back, right?

Cat   Maybe. No. We have Law.

Richard   Help I!

Cat   Yes.

(*She gets up to go.*)

Richard   Why? Why you help I?

Cat   You like us. Like Girl. See after.

Richard   Like Girl.

110   (*He sighs. **Cat** goes.*)

Richard Wish I never say coming, wish I never come. Boaster. She help I? Maybe, Maybe not. Cat. Stupid name.

(He lies down.)

Richard Cold.
Cold gold.
Cold.

SCENE 2

*(Early evening. The Making-Place in the village. **Grey**, one of the oldest women in the village, and **Wilder**, a younger woman, are making food-bowls. The eight girls we have already met are watching them.)*

Black You very old?

Grey Very, very old.

Black How old?

Grey Forty. In Old-Time, they sometimes live one hundred years.

Fox One hundred years!

Arrow When be Old-Time?

Wilder Long-Time ago.

Grey Long, Long-Time ago. Many Mothers ago.

Fox Old-Time Real-Time?

Willow Yes! Old-Time in Books, in Teaching!

Flinty Stories, but Real-Time.

Cat *(hesitantly)* Men still in Old-Time.

Grey Yes.

Cat Live with Women.

Grey Yes.

Cat Men very Bad.

Grey Men very Bad.

Bone *(laughing)* Me and Fox Men This-Day. And Flinty. Me and Fox get put in Home.

Wilder You playing Catch-Men?

Grey Catch-Men Old-Game.

Cat Grey . . . in Home, Men never see Sun. Never see Plant. Never walk, never run. From Boy-Babies till Last-Fire.

Grey So?

Cat Men so Bad?

(**Grey** *finishes her bowl. She has been asked this question many time before.*)

Grey Men have roof, clothes, covering. Get Food, some walking, some Sun. No Work. Only Breeding.

Arrow But Men not free.

Grey So? Men free in Old-Time. Men Leaders in Old-Time. Make bombs. And bombs making Bad-Time.

Wilder Men making Bad-Time.

Flinty Teaching say, Women Leaders too.

Grey Some. Copied Men. No choice.

Wilder And after Bad-Time, Men sorry? No! Still killing and killing and more killing.

Willow Cows for food.

Grey Each other for things.

Wilder Men Long-Away in other Nunkertowns, for more things.

Grey Fewer things so many more killing.

Wilder And Women still here. Breeding, Cooking, Cleaning, Teaching.

Grey And when Men come back, do *their* jobs, Planning and Building and Making, still no Peace.

Wilder Men from other Nunkertowns come here.

Grey Killing.

Wilder   So. One day . . .

Flinty   So few Men left . . .

Bone   Women catch them . . .

Fox   And put them in Home!

Grey   Now Men just for Breeding.

Wilder   And all Women Leaders. First Law Caring . . .

Cat   First Law Caring . . .

Wilder   Not killing. Have Peace. Do *all* jobs in turn . . .

Bone   Making Food-Bowls!

Grey   Share. Guard Edge. And other Nunkertowns Leave-Alone.

Black   So far.

*(Everyone looks at **Black**.)*

Cat *(quickly)*   Men born Bad?

Wilder   Some think yes, born Bad. Why we put Boy-Babies in Home.

Grey   Some think, part of Copying-Chain. Break chain, break copying.

*(There is a pause. Then **Cat** speaks, a little awkwardly.)*

Cat   Going walk. Good-Time After-Sun. Cool. Smell Plant.

(She takes a fire-pot.)

Cat   See after!

*(She goes. **Black** follows.)*

Black   See after.

*(**Arrow** slips out after **Black**.)*

Arrow   See after.

Riji   Something cook in their pot, Flinty.

Flinty   Black with new game maybe.

Riji   No. More than game. That Cat, she clear as Water. This-Day, Water rough. Trouble there.

Bone   Sing us, Wilder.

Fox   Yes, sing us.

(*Wilder finishes her bowl. She begins to sing.*)

Wilder   Old-Time, Women tall as sky,
  Old-Time, women straight and high,
  Giants.

  Old-Time, Women strong, but weak,
  Old-Time, Women strong, but meek,
  Wearing golden ornaments.

  Bad-Time come like Fire.
  Bad-Time come like Rain.
  Bad-Time come.

  Now-Time, Women stoop and creep,
  Now-Time, Women mourn, they weep
  For twisted limbs and backs.

  Now-Time, Women wear no gold,
  Now-Time, they look less than old,
  Weak, but strong.

  Bad-Time come like fire.
  Bad-Time come like rain.
  Bad-Time come no more.

Grey (*softly*)   Bad-Time come no more.

(*Silence.
  Suddenly there is a commotion. Two women run into the Making-Place; one is Willow's birth-mother, **Maze**, the other is **Moon**. They are guarders. They are both out of breath.*)

Grey   Maze. Moon. There be trouble?

Maze   Speak, Moon.

Grey   Get Water, Willow.

(*Willow fetches some water for **Maze**.*)

Moon   We find tunnel.

Fox Tunnel!

Moon Opening by Plant, longway Edge.

Wilder Outsiders coming?

Moon Maybe. We follow tunnel someway. Leading under Edge.

Fox Under Edge!

Moon Tunnel empty.

Maze Outsiders out – or in?

Fox In? In Village?

Maze Maybe.

Moon Maze light Fire as marker.

Maze Guarders go stand with Fire, watching. We Run-Tell, all
Women go now, leave jobs, hunt Outsiders.

**Wilder/
Grey** Coming.

(They prepare to leave.)

Flinty All Women?

Moon Young Women stay.

Maze Stay together.

*(She touches **Willow's** cheek. In a moment all four women are gone.)*

Fox Outsiders!

Bone Men maybe!

Willow In Village!

Fox First time.

Flinty Yes. First time. Edge is high wall, many on Guarding.
Outsiders Leave-Alone so far.

*(**Riji** repeats the words thoughtfully to herself.)*

Riji So far.

Bone Outsiders Leave-Alone high wall now! Come under, digging
like foxes.

Riji (*suddenly*)   Black say 'so far'!

(*They look at her.*)

Riji (*excitedly*)   Before-Time, Grey say, 'Other Nunkertowns Leave-Alone.' And Black say, 'So far'!

Flinty   Like she know.

(*There is a pause. They all think.*)

Fox   Black acting secret all This-Day.

Bone   And Arrow.

Riji   And Cat.

Flinty   Acting secret since Food-Time!

Bone   Since High-Sun!

Flinty   Since Cave-Place.

Willow   Cat save Food at Food-Time. See her bagging it.

(*They look at her.*)

Riji   Fire-Pot! She take Fire-Pot on walk 'After-Sun'. Sun-Fall long time yet!

Flinty   They go Cave-Place.

Fox   Feeding Man-Ghosts?

Flinty   No, Fox. Outsiders maybe.

Fox   Outsiders!

Willow   Men! Killers!

Flinty   No. Women-Outsiders maybe.

Riji (*slowly*)   No. Men-Outsiders. Cat All-Time talking Men.

(*They look at each other in horror.*)

Willow   Outsiders put in Home. Law say.

Flinty   Quick. All run Cave-Place.

Willow   Maze say all stay together.

Flinty   But not where stay together. We stay together, running Cave-Place! Begin.

(They leave the making-place at a run.)

SCENE 3

*(Early evening. **Cat, Arrow** and **Black** enter the mouth of the cave.)*

Cat   Richard. Richard!

(Silence)

Cat   Richard!

(He comes into the light.)

Richard   You bring others.

Cat   Bring food, bring covering.

(She hands them to him. He wraps the covering around him and starts to devour the food. Then he stops.)

Richard   You bring Village, right?

Arrow   No.

(He continues to eat.)

Arrow   You eat cows?

(He looks at her.)

Arrow   Meat?

Richard   You bet. Sheep. Pigs. Birds.

Black   You kill them?

(He looks at her warily now.)

Richard   Yes.

Black   How you kill them?

Richard   With knife.

*(He looks at **Arrow**. She still has his knife.)*

Richard   With hands. See?

(He demonstrates. They flinch slightly.)

Richard   How you?

Arrow   We do not kill. Eat growing things, plants, fruit.

(He shrugs.)

Richard   Meat good.

Cat   Where you live?

Richard   In valley, you know.

Cat   Tell. What like?

Richard   Hut, four walls, roof. We sleep on – like this.

(He points to the covering.)

Richard   My father, my mother, my brother.

Arrow   You live in fours?

Richard   Threes, fours. Families, right?

Arrow   Small. We live big. Tens. Twenties.

Richard   Big families, right?

Arrow   Big. All small Girls in Teaching-Place with Teachers. All Makers in Making-Place, Cooks in Cooking-Place, Growers in Growing-Place.

Cat   Change job, change place.

(There is a pause. She thinks.)

Cat   Right?

(The others look at her.)

Richard   What job you on?

Cat   No job. After-Teaching now, wait First-Blood, becoming Woman. Free now.

Richard   You easy time.

(He has finished eating.)

118   **Cat**   What job you on?

Richard   I work All-Time, all jobs. Else I hit.

Black   Hit?

(He demonstrates.)

Richard   Father hit I, right? *(He shrugs.)* Mother hit I.

Black   Your Birth-Mother?

Cat   Why you Want-Go home?

Richard   My home good.

(He looks at her.)

Richard   You shut I away, right?

Black   Yes.

Cat   No.

Black   Yes. Be Law for Men. Men, Killers.

Cat   Not Man. Boy.

Black   Same. Killers.

Richard   No.

Cat   Part of Copying-Chain.

*(**Richard** doesn't understand.)*

Cat   Break chain, break copying.

*(**Black** doesn't answer.)*

Cat   First Law, Caring.

*(They look at **Richard**.)*

Arrow   You look Girl. In Books, Men look Men.

Richard   Soon voice crack.

Arrow   Crack?

Richard   Go more deep. And beard grow. Like Father, right?

(He gets up and struts about in the blanket, walking like his father. They laugh. He speaks in his father's voice.)

Richard   Richard. Come here. I say come here, right? Give brother his stone back. You, woman, bring pipe!

*(They laugh so much they do not hear **Riji** and the others run in.)*

Riji   See here!

Bone   Outsider!

*(The four stop laughing and whirl round, horrified. **Richard** speaks to **Cat**.)*

Richard   I trust you. You bring others.

Cat   No!

Fox   Cat not tell.

Bone   We find you.

Willow   Call Guarders.

*(She turns to leave the cave. **Cat** stops her.)*

Cat   No!

*(**Black** joins her.}*

Black   Wait!

Flinty   You Bad; Cat, Arrow, Black. Women trust you. You break Law.

Cat   No!

Arrow   Just talking.

Cat   You talk, Flinty. His name Richard.

Riji   No. Call Guarders.

Cat   They shut him in Home. Flinty. Flinty!

Willow   Me call them.

(She takes out her whistle.)

Black   Willow!

Arrow   Wait!

Willow   No.

(She blows the whistle: the sound is piercing.)

Richard   No!

*(He tries to bolt. **Riji** and **Willow** stop him. He runs to **Cat**.)*

Richard   They shut I away. They kill I. Help I!

Cat   Let him go back. Back over Edge. He not come again.

Richard   No. Not come back, never, never!

Cat   See? Let him go!

Richard   Let I!

*(He runs to **Fox**.)*

Fox *(frightened)*   Flinty!

Flinty   Boy, Leave-Alone!

*(He runs to **Bone**.)*

Bone   Help! Help!

*(**Maze, Moon, Grey** and **Wilder** enter the cave.)*

Moon   Here!

Maze   Get him.

*(**Moon** and **Wilder** seize **Richard**.)*

Grey   Boy-Child.

Maze   He has knife?

Arrow   No. Me take it.

Maze   Take him Village.

Wilder   Come, Boy.

Grey   You play Catch-Man This-Day. Oh yes.

*(They leave with **Richard**. **Cat** cries.)*

SCENE 4

(Next day. The Teaching-Place. The women of the village are having a 'meet' elsewhere to decide **Richard's** *fate. Two women,* **Stone** *and* **Flight**, *cannot go because they are on teaching and must look after the younger girls. They have already given in their votes. The young women, who cannot vote either, have joined them at the Teaching Place.)*

Fox How you vote, Flight?

Flight Same as Stone.

Fox How you vote, Stone?

Bone Same as Flight.

(They laugh.)

Fox Me think they kill him.

Flight No. Him Boy-Child only.

Willow Him have knife.

Cat Richard hurting no-body.

(They look at her.)

Flight No. Him not killing. Women not kill unless being killed.

Stone But not let him go back over Edge. He find way here, he see things, he learn things. Go back, tell more Outsiders . . .

Flight More Outsiders come.

Arrow You think they put him in Home?

Stone Best thing.

Cat Richard be there till he die. Till Last-Fire.

Flight Same all Men.

Cat This more Bad. Richard Outsider, not from here. Not in Home All-Time, from Boy-Baby. Richard know running and walking and being free. More losing.

(They look at her.)

Stone Things changing anyhow. Changing like Weather. No stopping it. Men in Home getting less.

Flight   Women Breeding less.

Stone   Less Girl-Babies.

Flight   Not enough Women for Villages.

Stone   Villages getting small.

Bone   So, After-Day, maybe one Woman be Village!

Flight   Or no Woman.

Stone   Villages dying. Not enough Women for jobs. Not enough Women on Guarding, Outsiders coming anyway! See, one find us This-Day.

Flight   Some think, let Outsiders in.

Willow   No!

Black   Even Men?

Flight   Women. Men. New Men, new Breeding. More Children.

Riji   Living with Men!

Flinty   Like Old-Time.

Cat *(excitedly)*   Maybe Outsiders come in, copy Women in *Now-Time*, not Men in Old-Time. New Copying-Chain! No more killing!

Stone *(slowly)*   Once, in Old-Time, some Good places, some Good islands, have Peace like us. No killing, no bombs.

Arrow   Women-Places?

Stone   Men-and-Women Places. And Men come in from other places, take land, kill people, make people slaves, give disease. Bad not copy Good Before-Time. Bad not copy Good now.

Flight   Bad not changing. Outsiders not change for us.

*(**Maze**, **Grey** and **Wilder** enter.)*

Flinty   Meet finish?

Grey   Meet finish.

Riji   What you do?

*(The new arrivals look at **Stone** and **Flight**. **Wilder** cannot speak for anger.)*

Maze   We send him back.

Flight   Back?

Maze   Over Edge.

Stone   Over Edge!

Flight   Telling more Outsiders!

(They are angry.)

Grey   We talk Long-Time. Long-Time. Many, many things.

*(**Wilder** finds her voice at last.)*

Wilder   It is ending. Good-Time.

Grey   Maybe. Maybe not.

*(**Wilder** shouts.)*

Wilder   It is ending!

*(**Moon** enters leading **Richard**. She looks at the young women.)*

Moon   He Want-Speak with you.

Richard   They let I go home.

Black   Yes.

Richard   I Come-Say goodbye, right?

Black   Yes. Goodbye.

(The word 'goodbye' is new to her.)

Arrow   Yes. See after.

(The others look at her.)

Arrow   No. Goodbye.

(She gives him back his knife.)

Cat   Goodbye.

*(The others will not speak. **Richard** looks at **Cat**.)*

Richard See after.

(*Moon* *takes him to the door.*)

Moon Me cover eyes now.

Richard No. Wait.

(*He runs to* **Cat**.)

Richard I give you this. (*He gives her something.*)

(**Richard** *is blindfolded and taken away.* **Cat** *is left looking at the knife.*)

A Vocabulary of Nunkertese Words

After-Day	Another, a later day.
After-Sun	Evening, night-time.
After-Teaching	The time when young Girls have finished their education in the Teaching-Place, but have not yet become adult Women. During this time, they are not expected to work.
All-Time	All the time, always.
Animal-Place	Animal lair.
Bad-Time	The nuclear holocaust.
Before-Day	Yesterday.
Before-Time	Earlier.
Birth-Mother	A Girl's mother by birth, but not the Woman who has raised her, as all Girls are raised by Teachers in the Teaching-Place, and these change at intervals according to a rota.
Breeding-Time	The time once a year when adult Women visit the 'Home' in their Nunkertown in order to try to conceive female children.
Catch-Men	A game like Hide and Seek. The Hiders are called 'Men' and the Seekers are called 'Catchers'. 'Catchers' count up to twenty while the 'Men' hide, and may not start looking for them until the count is up. If the 'Men' are caught they get tossed into 'Home' to a ritual rhyme. If they escape to a safe spot called 'Edge', they go free. Like 'Ring a Ring o' Roses' in this country, this game is rooted in the history of its people.
Cold-Time	Winter.

Cross-World	Another of the Girls' games, this one played while travelling. One girls chants the rhyme, and whoever it finishes on (with the word 'out') loses the use of a limb, but chooses where the rhyme begins again. Limbs are lost in the following order – arm, other arm, leg and other leg, until eventually, players are limbless. The person with most limbs intact on arrival at the destination wins. Like Catch-Men this game is possibly based in the people's post-holocaust history.
Diggers	Spades and shovels.
Edge	The boundary of this Nunkertown, separating it from the others. It is marked by a high wall and strictly guarded against people from Outside – 'Outsiders' – coming in. In the game of Catch-Men, Edge is the only safe place for 'Men' running away from 'Catchers'.
Fire-Pot	A pot containing Fire, from which to light other Fires and torches. Saves having to make new Fire with flints or stones.
First-Blood	A Girl's first period, which marks her becoming a Woman.
Food-Time	Meal-Time.
High-Sun	Noon.
Home	'Home' for the Girls means the place where all Men are kept, and where all male babies are placed at birth. It is a prison, but treats its inmates unusually well. So, in the Girls' games, a dungeon, punishment or penalty area is usually called 'Home'.
Last-Fire	Cremation. The Women burn their dead.
Long/longer	Far/further.
Long-Time	A long time (ago).
Making-Place	Workshop accommodation for Women who are 'Makers', i.e. those who make all the artefacts (objects like cooking-pots, instruments) for their society.
Man-Place	A place which Men used in Old-Time.
Meet	Meeting.
Next-Day	Tomorrow.
Nunkertown	The word probably comes from 'non-contaminated area' (NonConTam) – though it has been suggested that it comes from the words 'Nuke Town'. Describes the large division of the country in which the characters live. It is not a town, more like a region or county, and contains some villages, and some uninhabited land.
Old-Time	The old days, when Men still lived in the community.

One-War	The way of counting seconds in games, again probably to do with the past history of the people in the Nunkertown.
On Guarding	Doing the job of a Guard.
On Teaching	Doing the job of a Teacher.
Outsider	Someone who lives 'Outside' the Nunkertown, beyond Edge, in another area of the country. May be female or male.
Plant	Probably from 'Plantation'. Means an area of cultivated land, where Food is growing.
Real-Time	History; real time as against a time in stories or games.
See after	See you later.
Short-Time	A short time, a little while.
Shut-Away Place	Prison.
Something cook in their pot	Something's going on.
Sun-Fall	Sunset.
This-Day	Today.

Talking Points

(For discussion in small groups, write each 'Talking Point' on a separate piece of card.)

1. Why does Richard give his knife to Cat?
What is she thinking as she watches him go?
Will he come back?
If he does, will he come as a friend or as an enemy?

2. The women had three choices at the 'meet': to kill Richard, to lock him up for life, or to let him return over Edge. Do you agree with their final decision?

3. There has been a nuclear war in Old-Time. What has changed? What has stayed the same?

Investigations

1. The writer has invented new-style names for the characters in this play. Spend some time looking at the names she has used. Now invent a new set of names for yourself and your classmates. Make them flattering, not abusive!!! What will your starting-point be? You could base the names on a person's skills: for example, Runner, Counter, Speller. You could use names of the streets where people live . . . King, High, Moordown. You could use your classmates' ambitions as a starting-point . . . Pop-star, Mechanic, Teacher. You will have your own ideas.

2. Invent a new language, which is based on your own, but which has slight differences. You'll need to write out a list of the most common words, just like the Nunkertese vocabulary list at the end of the play, and you'll also need to work out a set of rules for this new language. You might even want to replace written vocabulary with a set of picture symbols.
When you've worked out the rules and a basic vocabulary, write a letter to a friend . . . with an accompanying vocabulary to help them work out what it means.

3. (a) The writer has worked out a set of rules for Nunkertese, her invented language. In pairs, look back through the script, and see if you can work out what the rules are.
(b) If you look carefully, you'll see that Richard speaks in a different way to the girls. What differences can you find? You'll find evidence to back up your research on page 105.

4. Even in English there are many different ways of speaking. Different areas have different 'dialects'. Work with a partner and draw up a list of differences between your own way of speaking English, and the way that news readers on television might speak. Do you use words they don't use? Do you have rules for your language that are different from theirs?

5. We have a lot of words at our disposal. They're all there, just waiting to be used! Here's an exercise in word-building!

The aim is to write a poem about a world disaster. It can be a natural disaster, such as an earthquake, or one that's been caused by human beings. Choose the event that you want to write about, and then jot down five descriptive words that you could use in your poem. You can only have five, so make your selection carefully. Once you've written them down, hide the paper!

You'll need to decide now whether to work as a whole class, or in groups of about ten. You have a few minutes to move around and whisper your five words to as many people as possible in the group/class. They will whisper their words to you. When the time-limit is up, go back to your paper and write down the words you heard – as many of them as you can remember. If some of them are the same as the ones you've already written, leave them out.

It's now time to sit and write your poem, using as many words as you can from your new 'vocabulary bank'. You may find that having a new range of words can spark off a whole new set of pictures in your mind. Use the finished poems to mount a classroom display.

6. At the 'meet' some women wanted to kill Richard; others wanted to lock him up for life; others wanted to send him back over 'Edge'. Divide into three groups, each group to represent one of these views. In your group, rehearse the arguments you will use and then come together to discuss Richard's fate.

At the 'meet' you need to decide who will control the meeting. How will you make the final decision? Will everyone have a say?

After the 'meet' discuss what happened to group loyalties during the course of the discussion. Who presented their arguments most persuasively? What effect did this have on the final decision? Did everyone co-operate at the 'meet'?

7. In small groups, imagine that you have been given the powers to create a new society. What rules would you want to make – if you wanted rules? And what penalties would there be if someone broke the rules of the group?

Compare your list of rules with those of the other groups. Have you all come up with very different ideas? Is there any common ground?

8. In pairs, imagine that you have little or no language in common. Decide on a situation where the two of you might meet by chance; for example, at a bus stop, in a supermarket, in a launderette, or out jogging. One of you needs some kind of help. The only person who is around to help you is your partner . . . but he or she doesn't speak your language!

Decide which of you is the one who needs help. That person must take the final choice on the situation/place you are meeting.

How will you demonstrate the kind of help you need? Will your partner be able to understand your actions or will they lead the two of you into even more confusion?

9. Play Catch-Men and Cross-World. If you need to be reminded of the rules, you'll find them in the vocabulary list at the end of the play.

10. Draw or paint the landscape of the play. Build the pictures up into a class display or mural.

129

11. Design the costumes for a stage version of the play. Consider not only the look of the clothes but also their colours and the kind of materials you'd want to use.

What materials might be available in the Nunkertown?

Label your designs carefully so that they could be easily understood by your costume maker.

BASEMENT BARGAINS

Tony Coult

THE CHARACTERS

Anton Kramer, a medical attendant in the German army

Members of 'The Basement', young people between the ages of 12 and 15:

Anna Kramer, Anton's sister
Barbara Lang
Leni Mann (female)
Lotte Bauer (female)
Richard Wolff
Werner Reiner

Ellen Rees, from the British Red Cross
Captain Simon Davies, Royal Corps of Signals
Corporal Lennie Michaels, Royal Corps of Signals

Mrs Lenz ⎫
Mr Grunewald ⎬ neighbours in a block of flats

There are non-speaking parts for two British soldiers.

About this play

We are in a German city in 1945. The Second World War has been over for some months, and the city is occupied by the British army. Food is hard to come by and expensive. In Bismark Street, the school received a direct hit from a British bomb and is in ruins. But the school's boiler room wasn't damaged too badly. It's been taken over by a gang of young people who call themselves 'The Basement'. Some of them have lost their parents; some have run away. Their wartime experiences make them behave much older than you might expect.

It's late October. The weather is starting to turn cold.

NOTE: Most of the characters are German and are supposed to be speaking in their own language. But Ellen Rees, Captain Simon Davies and Corporal Lennie Michaels are actually speaking in English most of the time.

SCENE 1   WEDNESDAY

*(An Army jeep pulls up in the little park over the road from the school. The driver is **Corporal Lennie Michaels**. In the back seats are **Captain Simon Davies** and **Ellen Rees**.)*

Davies   That's Bismark Street School. They live underneath it, in the basement.

Rees   It's terrible . . .

Michaels   At least they've got something over their heads, Miss. There's thousands who haven't, and Winter's gonna be cold.

Rees   Who looks after them?

Davies   No one.

Rees   It's a disgrace! People in Britain don't have the first idea this is going on.

Davies   They'd probably say it's what they deserve for starting the war. Eh, Corporal?

Michaels   Not the kids' fault, sir. Can't blame the kids, can you?

Davies   Have you seen everything you want to see, Miss Rees? It must be lunch-time, my tummy's rumbling.

Rees   I'll need to come back and talk to them, Captain Davies.

Davies   Fine. OK, Lennie, back to barracks and a nice piece of beef!

*(The jeep drives off towards the British Army barracks. As it disappears round the corner, someone peers out from behind the rubble of the old bandstand. This is **Anton Kramer**. He's in his late teens, thin and stubbly. He wears a dirty Army greatcoat with all the badges ripped off, and he carries a bag. It's obvious that he doesn't want to be seen.)*

SCENE 2

(Inside the basement. It's dark, except where light comes through holes in the floor above, and from an old oil-lamp. The main part of the basement is dominated by an old boiler. It's not lit, but is surrounded by broken-up wooden desks and chairs, piles of old school books, and pictures of famous people, including Adolf Hitler. When it gets really cold, they will use these things as fuel.)

*In a corner, **Leni Mann** lies on a mattress, covered in scarves and old coats. She is ill. The rest of 'The Basement' are there: **Anna, Barbara, Werner, Richard** and **Lotte**. All except **Leni** sit or squat in a circle round a sack.)*

Anna   Let's see then!

*(**Werner** tips the sack onto the floor. A whole load of stuff they've just found, or stolen, or begged, falls out.)*

Werner   Whose is that thing?

Barbara   Mine.

Anna   What is it?

Barbara   Music-box. Got it from the old house up by the bridge.

(She winds it up. It plays 'O Tannenbaum'.)

Werner   Loada rubbish!

Barbara   Shut up, Werner, better than anything you've brought.

Lotte   So what? We can't eat it, we can't burn it, so what use is it?

Barbara   I told you, are you deaf? Sell it to the soldiers.

Lotte   Never!

Anna   What did you get, Lotte?

Lotte   Cabbage leaves.

Werner   You always get cabbage leaves!

Lotte   So? They make good soup.

Barbara   Who says?

Lotte   Why don't you get something we can trade?

Barbara   What, like your sewer-soup?

*(**Lotte** grabs a piece of wood and threatens **Barbara** with it.)*

Lotte   Shut it, Barbara, or I'll shut it for you.

Barbara   Cow.

*(**Lotte** swipes at **Barbara**. **Barbara** jumps backwards, stepping on the music-box with a crunch.)*

Anna   That's enough! Give me that, Lotte!

(*Anna* and **Lotte** *stare at each other for a moment. Then* **Lotte** *hands the piece of wood over.* **Werner** *picks up the broken music box.*)

Werner   Well it's worth sod-all now!

Barbara   Her fault.

Lotte   You just shut it!

Anna   Both of you shut it! Listen, if we fight among ourselves, there'll be no Basement. And if that happens, we could all end up starving to death. Or freezing. Lotte . . . why don't you go and make the soup?

Lotte   Don't order me about!

Werner   Go on. We're hungry.

Lotte   I'll do it for Leni.

Anna   What do we do with a broken music-box?

Richard   Give it me. I can try and mend it.

Barbara   Reckon you can?

Richard   Possible.

Anna   We'll sort the rest of this stuff after dinner. All right?

Barbara   One day we're gonna find something really good. A watch . . . or a camera that actually works. Something good we can sell the soldiers.

Anna   That'll be the day. I'm off upstairs for the water.

SCENE 3

(**Anna** *climbs up the stairs from the basement to the classroom. Most of the roof has fallen in. In the middle of the room, there are cans and buckets for collecting rain-water.* **Anna** *moves to pick them up, but hears a sound.*)

Anna   Who's there?

(*She listens. Perhaps she was mistaken. She picks up a bucket and turns to go back. Suddenly she finds herself facing a dark figure. She cries out with fright, and drops the bucket, spilling the water.*)

Anton   Ssshh!

Anna   What do you want? Get away!

Anton   Anna. It's me.

Anna   Who are you? I don't know you.

Anton   Anton. Your brother Anton. Don't you recognise me?

Anna   Anton . . . ? He was killed . . .

*(**Anton** steps forward into the light. **Anna** stares hard at him for a few moments.)*

Anna   Anton! I don't believe this . . . I never thought I'd see you again!

(They hug each other.)

Anton   I looked for the house but it's gone. Where are Mum and Dad?

Anna   The bombing . . .

Anton   Dead?

Anna   Yes. How did you find me?

Anton   I asked some kids. They all seemed to know about you.

Anna   Where are you living?

Anton   Nowhere. I've come to stay with you.

Anna   I'd have to ask the others. But don't worry, they'll say yes when I tell them you're my brilliant brother Anton! Come on!

Anton   No! Wait! You mustn't tell them who I am.

Anna   Don't be stupid, why?

Anton   I can't tell you, Anna. Trust me.

Anna   What am I supposed to call you then?

Anton   Call me Eduard. And say I'm an old friend, not your brother.

Anna   What?

Anton   Eduard Müller. Look, there's my identity card.

(He shows her a card.)

Anna   That's not your name! What's going on, Anton?

Anton   Please, Anna, trust me.

(She looks at him for a moment.)

Anna   Bring that water!

*(**Anton** picks up a bucket of water and follows **Anna** downstairs.)*

SCENE 4

*(Later that evening, a meeting of 'The Basement' is in progress. Everyone is there, including **Anton**.)*

Lotte   So what makes you think you can help 'The Basement'?

Anton   I was a medical orderly in the Army. I can help if someone is ill or has an accident.

Lotte   Leni's got the consumption in her lungs. Coughs blood up all the time. Could you help her?

Anton   As it happens . . . yes I can.

(He opens his bag and tips the contents onto the floor. There are tins of meat and fruit, bars of chocolate, some small boxes and bottles with red crosses on them.)

Anton   Special medicines. They'll help her get better. And the food will too.

('The Basement' members look in amazement.)

Werner   Look at that . . .

Leni   Where did it come from, all this stuff?

Anton   Oh . . . we were issued with them in the Army. Special rations.

Leni   This is American.

Anton   What?

Leni   This chocolate bar. It's American, not German.

Anton Oh?

Leni And those medicine bottles, they've got English writing on them.

Anton So what?

Leni You said you got them from *our* Army –

Anton I told you! Special rations! What's the matter? I could have got a fortune for this stuff on the black market. What's the matter with you people, don't you want me to help you?

Barbara Who cares whether it's Brit or Yank or comes from the Moon? Who cares, eh?

Werner So why do you want to join 'The Basement', soldier-boy?

Anton Other people say this is the best kids' gang in the city. And I know Anna, don't I?

Richard You can't just join without bringing something.

Anton Are you blind? What's all this stuff?

Lotte He means something you're good at.

Werner You any good at nicking?

Anton What?

Werner Nicking. Thieving. Can you do that?

Anton If I have to.

Werner Prove it!

Anton Prove what?

Werner People who join 'The Basement' have to do a test. *We* all did.

Barbara Get us something!

Lotte More food.

Richard No, something that's fun.

Barbara Wally!

Lotte We can't eat fun!

Anton   I'll do both if I can. Right? Now, who wants some chocolate?

*(**Anton** picks up one of the bars, unwraps it and breaks off a piece for each person. They haven't seen chocolate for years.)*

SCENE 5   THURSDAY

*(A block of flats at the other end of Bismark Street. **Corporal Michaels** drives up in the jeep, with **Ellen Rees** in the back. Outside the main entrance, **Mrs Lenz** and **Mr Grunewald** face each other.)*

Mr Grunewald   You let them in, you stupid old crone!

Mrs Lenz   Don't you call *me* names, Mr Grunewald! You're not a policeman any more.

Mr Grunewald   You left the front door open, didn't you?

Mrs Lenz   Senile old fool.

Mr Grunewald   What? What did you say?

Mrs Lenz   You heard.

Mr Grunewald   How dare you! If I wasn't a law-abiding citizen I'd . . .

*(He threatens **Mrs Lenz**. **Corporal Michaels** jumps out of the jeep.)*

Michaels   Oi! Oi, that'll do!

Mrs Lenz   See? See what you've done with your fat mouth? Brought the English in!

Mr Grunewald   They wouldn't be here if you hadn't left the front door unlocked, fool!

Michaels   I said shut it!

Mr Grunewald   What's he saying?

Mrs Lenz   I don't know. 'Stop shouting', I shouldn't wonder.

Mr Grunewald (*at **Corporal Michaels***)   Shouting? Me shouting? After what's happened to me, you want me to stop shouting?

Michaels   Gimme strength! Shutten your gobben! Give us a hand will you, Miss Rees. I can't speak their lingo.

Rees   What do you want me to say?

Michaels   Find out what all the hoo-ha's about will you?

Rees   The soldier wants to know what the problem is.

Mr Grunewald   It's time something was done – they should be punished, properly punished! Why don't the British do something?

Mrs Lenz   He's been robbed, young woman. It happens all the time. It's the young people, they're out of control.

Mr Grunewald   Give'em a taste of the horsewhip, that'd soon put a stop to it!

Rees   What was stolen? Can you tell us?

Mr Grunewald   My beautiful music, that's all, my lovely music! It's not right, the British are supposed to be in charge of law and order, why don't they do something?

Mrs Lenz   This sort of thing didn't go on while there was a war.

Mr Grunewald   And he struck me, look!

(*He waves at his head.* **Ellen Rees** *looks and sees a bad cut, which drips blood onto his collar.*)

Rees   Corporal Michaels. Quick! This looks nasty. Got any first aid?

(**Mr Grunewald** *collapses, shivering, onto the pavement.*)

SCENE 6

(*Later that afternoon, in 'The Basement'. An old wind-up gramophone is playing. There are opened tins on the floor.* **Leni** *sits close to the machine, her eyes closed, swaying to the music.*)

Anton   It's called 'Jazz'. American music.

Barbara   Jazz. Yeah, it's great.

Richard   The gramophone's good, Eduard. Where did you get it?

Anton   Look, you lot set me the test – I passed it. That's all that matters.

Richard   I just wondered –

Barbara   Well don't. It's great having a gramophone, eh Anna?

Anton   Well? Can I stay or can't I?

(**Anna** *stops the music.*)

Anna   What do you think? Do we let him stay?

Barbara   Yeah!

Anna   Lotte?

Lotte   As long as he doesn't just get toys. Few more tins'd be good.

Anna   Werner?

Werner   Maybe.

Anton   Maybe?

Werner   How do we know he's not a British spy?

Anton   Screw that! I hate the British – they killed most of my best mates.

Werner   We don't know anything about him.

Anton   Anna does.

Anna   Yes, I do. He's all right, Werner.

Werner   OK then. For now.

Anna   Richard?

Richard   If other people want him, then I don't mind.

Anna   What do *you* want? Yes or no?

Richard   Yes. I think so.

Anna   That'll have to do. Leni?

Leni   I don't feel sick all the time any more. That's thanks to him. So I think . . . yes.

Anna   And I say yes. Welcome to 'The Basement' . . . Eduard Müller.

(**Barbara** *puts the record on again and starts to dance.*)

SCENE 7   FRIDAY

(*Morning; in the basement. It's pouring with rain.* **Leni's** *not well again, so* **Lotte** *is staying in with her. She tries to feed* **Leni** *with cabbage soup.*)

Leni   I'm not hungry.

Lotte   You've got to.

Leni   I'm all right! I've had some of Eddy's medicine.

Lotte   Oh yeah, the American medicine. He still hasn't told you where it comes from?

(**Anna** *comes over to them.*)

Anna   I'm going out. There's a gang clearing rubble in South Street. I'll make a bit of money.

Leni   It's pouring, Anna.

Anna   Too bad. You keep well wrapped up, eh?

Leni   That's all I ever do, sit here.

Anna   I know. It'll get better.

Leni   It won't. Eduard's medicine won't last for ever, and I'll just be stuck in this hole being sick, and gobbing up blood till I die.

Anna   Don't talk like that, Leni.

Leni   I'll talk how I like, all right!

Anna   I'll see you later.

(**Anna** *goes to the steps, followed by* **Lotte**.)

Lotte   Anna?

Anna   What?

Lotte   About Eddy . . .

Anna   You voted for him, Lotte. We all decided.

Lotte I know he's your friend . . . but do you trust him? Really?

Anna Of course I do.

Lotte I know he's helped us, and Leni especially.

Anna So stop moaning will you. I'll be late.

Lotte Anna listen! Those medicines – Werner says they're not army at all. They're Red Cross, the stuff prisoners-of-war get. How did Eduard get them?

Anna Look, Lotte, Eduard is in 'The Basement' and if you don't like it you can take your nasty, suspicious little mind and clear out, right? I'm going to work.

(**Anna** *runs up the rain-soaked basement steps, and* **Lotte** *goes back to see how* **Leni** *is.*)

SCENE 8

(*That evening: in the basement. Everyone is there, eating* **Lotte's** *soup and the last of* **Anton's** *tins. All around them are the things they have stolen or found during the day.*)

Richard There's a new lot of English up by the railway station. They look sick to death.

Leni Want to go home, I expect.

Richard I sold the music-box to one of them.

Leni You didn't!

Richard After I fixed it up. It sounded good.

Leni What's an English soldier want with a music-box that plays German tunes?

Barbara He'll sell it, most like, for ten times as much. It's called business.

Lotte Anna, there's something I want to say –

Anna Lotte, if it's about what you said this morning . . .

Lotte (*interrupting*) I'm not the only one who's worried.

Anna If anything's bothering you about Anton, you can say it to his face.

Lotte Anton??

Anna I meant . . . Eduard. Say it to his face, not behind his back.

Lotte Is he your boyfriend? Is that why he's here?

Anna No he is not! And if you say another word about him you'll get my fist in your face!

Leni Oh . . . stop it . . . please . . .

*(**Leni** starts to cough. **Richard** moves to help her, and so does **Anton**. He holds her by the shoulders.)*

Anton Breathe slowly, Leni. Slowly . . . that's it . . . you're better . . . good . . . drink some water . . . there. Feeling better?

Leni Better. Thanks Eddy. You're a help.

Anton I'm going to have to find you some more of those antibiotics.

(She lets him hold her. Suddenly there's the sound of footsteps up above in the schoolroom.)

Barbara Someone's coming!

Lotte Sssh! Keep quiet!

*(Everyone freezes, except **Anton**. He grabs the gramophone and frantically searches for somewhere to hide it.)*

Anna What are you doing!

Werner Keep still!

Lotte Ssshh!

*(**Anton** opens the boiler door and stuffs the gramophone roughly inside. As boots are heard on the steps from the classroom, he squeezes in behind the boiler to hide. The boots belong to **Corporal Michaels**. In one hand he holds a drawn service revolver, in the other a torch, which he flashes around the basement.)*

Michaels Here we are, Miss. These are the poor sods they call 'The Basement'.

(*Ellen Rees* comes down the steps.)

Michaels   Right, you lot! Listen to what the lady tells you. She wants to help you. Helpen-sie. All right?

Barbara (*in a whisper*)   What's the soldier saying?

Lotte (*in a whisper*)   I think he's going to kill us.

(*Lotte* and *Barbara* hold hands, close to tears.)

Rees   Hello. My name is Ellen Rees, from the Red Cross. Corporal, please. That gun is putting them off.

(*Corporal Michaels* reluctantly puts the revolver back in its holster.)

Rees   As I was saying, I am from the Red Cross. One of my jobs is to find homes for people like you.

(*She waits for some response, but they just stare blankly back at her.*)

Rees   Do you understand what I am saying? Is my German clear enough for you?

(*Still no response. She raises her voice.*)

Rees   Do you understand me?

Anna   Yes. We understand.

Rees   Good. In a few days' time, we're going to start a register, of all the young people living rough. Like you. When we know who you are, and where you are, we'll try to trace your families. If . . . if, sadly, we don't find anyone, then we will try and find you *new* families.

Richard   We won't go.

Anna   Richard! Sssh.

Richard   We won't be slaves.

Rees   What do you mean? You're not going to be slaves.

Richard   You'll take us away and we'll be made to work for rich foreigners as slaves.

Rees   Who told you that?

144   **Werner**   It's true, you sell German children as slaves for rich people –

Lotte – and they beat you and tie you up at night in chains –

Barbara – and they feed you pigswill.

Rees I promise you, none of this is true. Look, you can't stay here. This place is filthy, and it's going to be a cold winter. I can see that that girl is ill. Do you want her to die?

Richard You're not taking her away! You're not taking Leni!

(*Richard is shaking with anger. Corporal Michaels steps forward, fingering his revolver nervously.*)

Michaels I wouldn't push it, Miss. You never know with these poor beggars.

Rees All right, Corporal, I can deal with this. We just want the best for you. You can't stay in this dreadful place forever. (*To Michaels.*) They don't trust me. Can we come back with someone who can reassure them. (*To 'The Basement'.*) We'll speak again, all right? Please trust me.

(*She looks at them, but they just stare back at her. She turns and goes up the stairs. As Corporal Michaels turns to go, he sees one of the records.*)

Michaels Hello . . . Duke Ellington . . . Great stuff. Gut! Ja? Ellington gut? Yeah?

(*No response.*)

Michaels All right, have it your own way.

(*He retreats up the steps.*)

Werner (*quietly*) Damn you!

Anna Maybe she meant it.

Barbara We're all right as we are.

Lotte She's right about the winter. What about Leni?

Leni I don't want to leave here. Especially if Eddy can find me more medicine.

(*Pause.*)

Lotte Where is he? Eddy?

(*Anton comes out from behind the boiler.*)

Anton   They give me the creeps.

Barbara   You've broken the gramophone.

Lotte   Yeah, why did you stuff it in the boiler?

Anton   I told you – I don't like Brits.

Barbara   Nor do we. So what? We don't run round like headless chickens and hide just 'cos a couple of British come down.

Lotte   You'll have to get us another gramophone now.

Anton   Shut it, will you!

(He runs up the steps and out of the building.)

Barbara   Well well.

Lotte   I told you, Anna, I told you! Something's not right with him.

Anna   Don't start that again.

Richard   What? What do you mean, Lotte?

Werner   Sssh.

*(He points towards **Leni** who has fallen into an exhausted sleep. **Anna** pulls on her coat and leaves the basement.)*

SCENE 9

*(Later that evening, **Anton** is sitting alone in the classroom. **Anna** comes in, carrying a bag. At first, **Anton** doesn't hear her. As she goes slowly towards him, he looks up suddenly.)*

Anton   Checking up on me?

Anna   No.

Anton   They want me out.

Anna   Don't be stupid. They've only just got you in.

Anton   They don't like me.

Anna   They don't understand you. Like today. Sticking the gramophone in the boiler and hiding. What was all that about?

Anton Nothing.

Anna Oh yes it was. Why did you have to hide? Why didn't you want them to see the gramophone?

Anton Stop getting at me, Anna!

Anna You don't let me say you're my brother. I can't even call you Anton. Then you bring in all that American stuff. And you won't say where you got it. You hide like a rat when two Brits come in. What's up Anton?

Anton You're my sister, Anna! Trust me!

Anna How can I trust you if you won't trust me? Tell me what you're running away from, or I'll tell them who you are!

*(**Anton** is silent, then he decides to tell her.)*

Anton All right. It was in France. My unit was retreating from American tanks. We had about twenty Yankee prisoners with us. The Captain said we had to do something difficult, but that we owed our loyalty to him and Germany. We trusted him, our Captain. He said there was a problem with the prisoners. He said they slowed us down. We couldn't let them go. They'd tell the Yank Army which way we went. He said the problem had to be removed . . .

Anna You killed them? . . . You killed unarmed prisoners!

*(**Anton** is in tears now, but he carries on.)*

Anton I didn't fire the machine-guns, Anna. But after it was finished, the Captain told us medics to find out the ones who were still alive . . . And then he gave us all pistols and told us to shoot them dead.

Anna That was the war, Anton. It's over now. Forget it.

Anton After we'd dug the hole and put the dead Yanks in, the Captain came round and told us we were good loyal Germans and should be proud of ourselves and our country.

Anna Who's Eduard Müller?

Anton A lad in another unit who'd copped it. I took his papers the day we surrendered. I knew they'd be out to get our lot when they found the Yanks.

Anna   So, our medicines and food . . . belong to those prisoners?

Anton   If the British ever find out who I am, I'm dead. They'll put a rope around my neck for what I've done.

(***Anna*** *hugs him.*)

Anna   They won't find out.

(*But as she looks up, she finds herself staring at* **Lotte**, *who is standing by the stairs to the basement.*)

Anna   What are *you* doing?

Lotte   I've been looking after Leni.

Anton   You were spying!

Lotte   No . . . Leni wants you, Eddy.

(***Anton*** *looks at her, then quickly goes down the steps.* ***Anna*** *looks hard at* ***Lotte***.)

Lotte   Sorry. Did I interrupt something?

Anna   Just talking.

Lotte   To your friend?

Anna   That's right. Anything wrong?

Lotte   No. Nothing wrong. Nothing at all.

SCENE 10   SATURDAY

(*Morning; in the basement.* **Barbara, Werner, Richard** *are listening to* **Lotte**.)

Barbara   So what if he is Anna's brother? So what if he *did* kill some Yanks? We were fighting them weren't we?

Werner   Why can't he be straight with us?

Lotte   'Cos he's got something to hide!

Richard   Why don't we tell him we know who he is?

Lotte   I've got a better idea.

Barbara   We're not chucking him out!

Lotte   We swap him.

Barbara   We're not playing marbles, Lo.

Lotte   Listen! There's a lot of things we need here, right? Especially with winter coming.

Werner   So what?

Lotte   The British have got what we need. Medicines for Leni. Food. If we go and ask for it straight, they'll say, 'Yes, put Leni in our hospital', or, 'Yes, go and live where the Red Cross woman tells you'. And we know what that means.

Richard   The end of 'The Basement'.

Lotte   Right. So we go to Davies and say to him: 'Look, we know where there's someone you're looking for, someone who killed Yank soldiers after they'd been made prisoners'. We make a bargain with Davies: he gives us what we want – food and medicines. We give him what he wants: a War Criminal! Easy.

Barbara   What makes you think Davies would do all that?

Lotte   Obvious! It'll make him look good. My dad was in our Army. They're all like that.

Richard   What about Anna?

Lotte   She'll have to decide, won't she? Does she stick up for 'The Basement'? Or her brother who's gonna get caught and strung up sooner or later in any case.

Werner   We don't have to tell her anyway.

Lotte   You agree we should do it then?

Werner   Sounds good to me.

Lotte   Richard?

Richard   Betray him to the British? I'm not sure. He is a German, after all.

Werner   You want him here? Around Leni all the time? If we do Lotte's plan, you get rid of him, *and* you get all the stuff to make Leni better.

Richard   I'm not sure. We voted him into 'The Basement'.

Werner You're just a born coward!

Barbara Leave him alone!

Lotte We've got to be all together on this. One person steps out of line and it won't work. Barbara?

Barbara You don't like Eduard do you?

Lotte I don't give a damn about him. I *do* give a damn about 'The Basement', about *us*. So should you.

Barbara What does Leni think?

Lotte I'm not going to ask Leni. She'll say she doesn't want Anton in trouble just because she's ill. It only needs us four, and we can do it. What do you say?

Barbara All right. For 'The Basement'.

Lotte Richard? For Leni?

Richard Yes. For Leni.

SCENE 11

*(That afternoon. **Corporal Michaels** and **Ellen Rees** are sitting in the jeep in the park opposite the school. At the far end of the park, they can see **Captain Davies** talking to **Lotte** and **Werner**.)*

Rees What's your Captain doing now, Corporal?

Michaels Those kids? He gets info off them. Surprising how far a bar of Fry's chocolate goes in this dump. They're probably telling him something about one of the other gangs.

Rees Why does he want to know that?

Michaels He keeps in with the Military Police. He's like that, is Captain Davies; a bit of a slimy toad.

Rees He's finished talking to them. He's looking pleased about something.

Michaels Some little deal he's managed to pull off.

Davies *(approaching)* Start her up, Corp. It's freezing out here.

(He arrives at the Jeep and climbs in.)

Davies   I think we've solved your problem getting those kids into homes, Miss Rees.

Rees   Why? What have you done, Captain?

Davies   Oh just a little deal. We'll go there tomorrow. They'll sit up and listen like good little boys and girls.

Rees   Really? You're obviously in the wrong job, Captain Davies. You should be in the Red Cross finding homes for refugee children.

Davies   Me? Oh I've got better things to do than nursemaid German tearaways. Eh, Corporal?

Michaels   Yes sir.

Davies   Let's go then.

(*The jeep drives off towards the British barracks.*)

SCENE 12   SUNDAY

(*In the basement, they're having a lie-in. Church bells sound from the tower of the church near the park.*)

Lotte   What time is it?

Anton   Time they switched those damn bells off – I'm trying to sleep.

Richard (*whispers*)   Leni – I want to speak to you.

Leni   I'm listening.

Richard   Whatever happens today . . .

Leni   Get on with it!

Richard   It's for you.

(***Richard** gets up and goes to another part of the basement.*)

Leni (*to herself*)   What's he on about? Idiot!

(***Lotte** and **Barbara** talk quietly. **Lotte** is obviously nervous.*)

Barbara   Relax! Anna will guess something's up. Or Eddy will!

Lotte   He won't, look at him. He's asleep.

Barbara   All right, but relax will you?

Lotte   Stop going on at me to relax!

Werner   Have you mended that gramophone?

Richard   Course I have.

Werner   Let's hear it then.

Richard   Not until it's time.

Werner   Bet it doesn't work, anyway. Crap old machine!

Richard   I spent all last night mending it, Werner, so it bloody well *does* work, all right!

Werner   Keep your hair on, Ricky-Dicky.

*(He ruffles **Richard's** hair roughly. **Richard** jumps up, threatening **Werner** with a screwdriver.)*

Richard   Don't touch me, Werner Reiner, or else!

Werner   Take it easy, brainy-boy.

*(**Anna** comes over.)*

Anna   What's up? Why's everyone so jumpy?

(No one answers.)

Anna   You've fixed the gramophone, Richard?

Richard   Nothing was broken, except the horn. I glued it back on.

Anna   Eddy's going to be pleased.

Richard   Is he? Good!

Anna   Let's wake him up now.

Richard   No!

Anna   Why?

Barbara   Not till the bells stop ringing. It'll spoil it, having that row going on at the same time.

SCENE 13

(Outside, in the Park. **Michaels, Rees** *and* **Davies** *sit in the jeep. The bells echo all around.)*

Davies   Wait till the bells stop ringing, if you don't mind, Miss Rees.

Rees   I don't understand. Why don't we just go in if they're all there?

Davies   We'll do it my way, if you don't mind.

Rees   Oh this is silly, I'm going in now.

Davies   No! I know these kids, and if I make an arrangement with them, I expect to keep it. The bells stop at 11 o'clock. That's when you can go in.

Rees   I don't see why it's necessary to treat this like some kind of military operation.

*(**Davies** doesn't hear this. He is looking over at the clumps of trees nearby.)*

SCENE 14

(In the basement. **Anna** *and* **Richard** *are sorting through a pile of records.)*

Anna   What about this one? 'Minnie the Moocher'.

Richard   Er, no, not that one.

Anna   'Creole Love Call'?

(Suddenly the bells stop. **Richard** *looks awkwardly around.* **Barbara** *nods her head quickly.)*

Richard   All right. Give us it.

(He puts 'Creole Love Call' on the gramophone and winds it up. The music starts. **Anton** *stirs.)*

Anton   Shut up, will you? I'm trying to sleep here!

Anna   Don't be so ungrateful, you! They've mended your gramophone for you. It's a surprise!

Anton   Oh . . . sorry . . .

(*Anna* *notices something odd about the way the others are standing. The record plays on. No one hears the footsteps on the basement steps.*)

Rees Er . . . hello.

(*Everyone freezes.*)

Rees Don't worry. It's only me. Remember? The lady from the Red Cross. Ellen Rees.

(*Anton* *sits bolt upright. He's like a trapped animal.* *Lotte* *takes the needle off the record.*)

Rees Captain Davies tells me that you've had another think about your futures? And — which one's Leni? Are you Leni? — we can definitely find you a place in a hospital.

Leni I'm not going anywhere. You're not taking me away!

Rees But your friends here said . . .

(*Suddenly a whistle blows upstairs in the schoolroom. There's a clatter of boots on the steps.* *Captain Davies,* *followed by* *Corporal Michaels* *and two other soldiers come down the steps.*)

Davies Nobody move!

Rees Just a minute —

Davies Sorry about this, Miss Rees.

(*Richard* *moves.*)

Davies I said stand still!

(*He levels his revolver at* *Richard.*)

Anna What is this?

Rees Captain, I object to this!

Anna We've done nothing wrong!

Davies No? Then what's that?

(*Davies* *points at the gramophone.*)

Davies Anyone know a Mr Grunewald? Nice old chap. Liked music, used to have a gramophone just like that one. Trouble is, he can't hear anything now. Not after someone hit him on the head.

Rees You should have told me about this, Captain Davies!

Davies Which one of you is Anton Kramer?

Rees Did you hear what I said?

*(**Anton** slowly gets up. He looks accusingly at **Anna**.)*

Anna Anton . . . I didn't know.

Davies Corporal Michaels . . . take him out.

*(**Michaels** moves to tie **Anton's** hands. But **Anna** moves first.)*

Anna No!

*(She rushes at **Davies**. **Anton** reacts instantly, leaping for the staircase. **Davies's** revolver goes off, firing at the ceiling. **Michaels** and the two soldiers run after **Anton**. **Davies** recovers himself, pushing **Anna** back amongst the others. For a moment the only noise is **Leni's** crying.)*

Davies You'll regret doing this.

(Outside, a shot is heard, and a cry of pain.)

Rees Stop them! Stop the shooting!

Davies It's stopped, I reckon.

Rees You used me, Captain Davies, you used me to catch a common thief.

Davies You think that's what he is, do you?

Rees You lied to me. How are these kids going to listen to me now?

Davies I had my reasons, as you'll find out.

Rees You'd better have! Because I'm going to create such a stink about this, you won't know what hit you!

*(She storms up the steps. **Davies** looks at 'The Basement' kids cowering. He speaks to **Anna**.)*

Davies Don't worry. My men were instructed to disable, not to kill. More than can be said for his lot.

*(**Davies** turns and goes up the steps. He stops. A moment's silence, except for **Leni's** crying.)*

Davies Cheer up. We get our man. You get your medicines. A deal is a deal.

(He goes. For a while no one says anything.)

Leni They say they did it for me, Anna . . . I would have stopped them if I'd known . . .

Anna They? Who's they?

Lotte It was our decision, Anna.

Anna You! I should have guessed!

*(She moves threateningly towards **Lotte**. But then she stops, waits and finally grabs her bag, stuffs her few belongings in it, and runs up the steps. **Leni** calls after her.)*

Leni Anna!

SCENE 15   MONDAY

*(Early morning. A room in the British barracks, empty except for a chair, a table, and a photo of the King on the wall. There are bars on the window because this used to be the city's gaol. **Ellen Rees** stands by the window staring out. The door opens. **Corporal Michaels** shows **Anna** into the room.)*

Michaels Sit down.

Rees Thanks Corporal.

Michaels You be all right in here?

Rees I'll call you when we're ready.

*(**Corporal Michaels** goes out.)*

Rees Have they told you what's going to happen?

Anna They're going to put him on trial. Then I expect they'll hang him.

Rees He'll get a fair trial, Anna. What he did was –

Anna What he did was what he was ordered. I want to go now.

Rees I can still help you. I could arrange for you to stay near your brother.

Anna You said you wanted to help us before . . . and look what happened!

Rees   I didn't know about –

Anna   Don't believe you!

Rees   It's true, Anna. I swear!

Anna   I want to go now.

Rees   Where? Where will you go?

Anna   I don't know. Anywhere away from here. Let me out!

(***Anna*** *stands and goes to the door.* ***Ellen Rees*** *opens it.*)

Rees   We're ready to go, Corporal Michaels.

(***Corporal Michaels, Rees*** *and* ***Anna*** *walk through the building, along corridors and down stairs.*)

Rees   Did 'The Basement' kids get their side of the bargain, Corporal?

Michaels   The medicines and stuff? In the end, yes. Davies wasn't going to keep his side of things. But he soon changed his mind.

Rees   What happened?

Michaels   Look . . . he's always using Army food and drugs to bribe civilians with. If he was caught, he'd end up in jail, right? So, he tried to wriggle out of the bargain with the kids.

Rees   What changed his mind?

Michaels   I told him I'd shop him at Anton's trial. I'd tell the court about all his little deals and tricks. Davies got the message all right.

Rees   Aren't you taking a risk? He's an officer. You're not.

Michaels   Maybe! But what he was doing was wrong. Why should I be loyal to a man like that?

(***Michaels, Rees*** *and* ***Anna*** *have arrived at the door to the street. Before anyone can stop her,* ***Anna*** *runs through it.* ***Rees*** *calls after her.*)

Rees   Anna! Anna!

Michaels   I'll get her back.

Rees   No! Don't! It's up to her what she does now.

SCENE 16

*(Later that day, **Anna** walks along Bismark Street, carrying a bundle. She arrives at the ruined school. She stops for a moment. Jazz music comes up the steps from the basement. At that moment **Anna** knows that she must either go down the steps, or start her life somewhere else. Will she be loyal to her brother? Or to 'The Basement'?)*

Talking Points

(For discussion in small groups, write each 'Talking Point' on a separate piece of card.)

1. What does Anna do at the end of the play? Does she keep walking along Bismark Street, or go down the stairs to the basement?

2. The members of 'The Basement' had each made a decision to let Anton stay, and yet – with the exception of Anna and Leni – they all inform on him. Do you think they had good reasons for doing so?

3. What kind of loyalty made Anton shoot unarmed prisoners? Do you think Anton got what he deserved?

4. Why does the British officer Michaels trick Ellen Rees? Do you think he had good reasons for doing this?

Investigations

1. When Anton comes to join 'The Basement', he is told that one of the rules is that he can't join without bringing something.

What do you think the other rules might be?

Write out a list of these rules for the members of 'The Basement'.

2. Ellen Rees tells 'The Basement' that the Red Cross will soon start making a list (a register) of all the youngsters living rough in the city. Imagine that she also writes a report (to go with the list) which paints a vivid picture of the life these children lead in this ruined city. What suggestions might she make for improving the situation? Use these headings for her report: Food and water; Sleeping conditions; Hygiene and health; Morale.

3. In quiet moments, each member of 'The Basement' has started a notebook of his or her experiences. Put yourself in the place of one of the characters and write a page from your notebook. You could write it as a diary entry, or a short story, or a poem. Whatever you choose, let it show how you feel about your life in this place.

4. Anton will be put on trial as a war criminal. He has been accused of taking part in the killing of unarmed prisoners. His defence will be that he was simply carrying out orders. He was being loyal to his captain and to his country.

You have the job of preparing the final speech for or against Anton's actions. Present your speech to the court (the class?).

You may need to check back through the script (particularly pages 147 and 148) to help you prepare evidence to support your argument.

5. At the end of the play, Anna stands at the door of the basement, not knowing what to do next.

In threes, work out a scene which shows what the voices in her head might be saying at that moment. One voice will urge her to be loyal to her brother. The other will tell her that she has new loyalties to her basement 'family'.

What will Anna say to both of them; and what will she decide to do?

6. Let's say that Anna chooses to go back to 'The Basement'. In groups, work out a scene which shows what happens when she walks down the stairs and meets the others for the first time since her brother's arrest.

Compare each group's version of the event. Do the characters in each of the versions react in similar or different ways?

7. Work out and show a series of 'photographs' which illustrate how the members of 'The Basement' survive in the ruins of the city. How do they get food; how do they avoid capture; what measures do they take to keep their hiding place secret?

You'll need to work in small groups, with each group planning three or four situations to show. Become the people in the 'photographs', and when you show your photographs to the rest of the class, move from one 'photograph' to the next at an agreed signal. You may want to give your 'photographic' collection a suitable title.

If you can find pictures of British or German cities in the period immediately following the end of the Second World War in 1945, they may help you to build up a clearer idea of the setting for *Basement Bargains*.

8. Draw a floor plan of the basement, showing where everyone sleeps, where the stairs are, how much space is taken up by the boiler etc. Look back through the script to help you make your plan as detailed as possible.

9. The city is under army control. Life would be a lot easier if you had a set of identity papers – real or forged!

Make an identity card or passport for one of the people in 'The Basement'.

You'll need to provide details of that person's name, age, date of birth, place of birth, parents' names etc. You could sketch in a 'photograph' or cut one from a magazine.